God is Great
But His People Suck

(For the dainty hearted
please cut along line)

A Polemical Look at Life With a
Propitious Twist; Written by a Pleb

Brad Shiff

God is Great But His People Suck
A Polemical Look at Life With a Propitious Twist;
Written by a Pleb
Copyright © 2017
Authored by Brad Shiff

Scripture is mainly from the ESV version of the Holy Bible with verses from other versions.

Book design by Brad Shiff.

Acknowledgments:

Special thanks to the editors who took my scattered thoughts and reshuffled them to be readable:

- Alexandra Shepherd
- Hayley Dupree
- Jeff Dupree
- Blaine Shiff
- Eric England
- Olivia Shiff
- and "A"

Especially special thanks to my daughter, Alexandra Shepherd. Without her persistence this book would not have started. Even though the words and stories are from my experiences, I consider her a co-author. Alexandra prompted me to start it with a trip to Vegas, and her cheerful guidance saw it through to the end. Alexandra's reminders, encouragement, support, suggestions, editing and unquantifiable amounts of time... while she raises her young son, were precious to me.

Dedications:

- God- without Him, writing a book would be rather difficult... since I wouldn't exist.
- Jesus- for paying my penalty.
- Holy Spirit- for guiding and guarding me.
- Mom, Dad, Blaine, Heather, Natalie (my beautiful wife), Alexandra, Roman, Lander, Carter, Waverly, Alex, John, Hiram, Dave, Tim, Eric, Matt, Lou, Faye, Gertrude, Sarah, Frank, Don, my other relatives and friends... and every other person I have ever met, read, heard, or watched... because you also help shape who I am.

Important Notes:

- To those who are hurting- please reach out. Let people know so they can help. Be patient and honest. If you think we can help, contact us at: team@LifeisHarsh.com

- If you appreciate this book and would like us to speak at your school, university, church, or any other venue, please contact us at: speak@LifeisHarsh.com

Contents:

WARNING

This book has the potential to offend. Christians, I use naughty words. Non-Christians, I cite Bible verses, so don't freak out. Scientists, I challenge your superior-than-thou ways. Feminists, I use generic words like mankind. This book may take people out of their comfort zone. If you are easily triggered, you may want to take a couple puffs on your inhaler and read it in your safe space… with your favorite stuffed toy… and a mug of warm cocoa. This book is about love. True love. Not today's feel-good, lovey-dove love. So, feel free to think, laugh, and cry with me as you read this book.

1

I Don't Like Christians

Call me Brad. I'm a pleb. An ordinary person in a lifelong struggle searching for truth. I consider myself among the greatest of sinners since I have come to believe in God and His Word. When I know better, I should be better. God expects more of me, even in the "small" sins like impatience or jealousy. This book may seem harsh, but the goal is to seek and speak the truth which may result in unintended offense. If you do get offended, I say, "Good!" They're just words, so suck it up, buttercup, and read on!

I must confess that I generally don't like Christians, which immediately presents a problem: I am one. *Sigh.* I like hippies, free thinkers, and honest truth seekers regardless of whether they believe what I believe. They are searching life's answers, which is exactly what God asks people to do, (Jeremiah 29:13, Matthew 7:7, James 4:8). I grew up "churchized" and learned to speak fluent "Christianese." Eventually, church wore me down with its monotonous routines week after week after mundane week. Christians robotically cited the "Lord's prayer" and blithely sang songs without a care or thought to the words, while the offering plate was dutifully passed. Sermons preached sounded more and more like Charlie Brown's teacher, which caused intellectual and spiritual emaciation. Church helped me to become *dispassionate* about God by teaching simple stories without showing how to intellectualize, practically apply, or adequately defend them. But this is not a wholesale indictment of all churches; there were and are many outstanding aspects of the church and I made lifelong friends with whom I am still in touch with weekly. Christians, you may be saying, "Maybe he grew up in a lousy church but *mine* was supercalifragilisticexpialidocious!" My experience through five decades in numerous churches is that they are boringly similar and make God seem prudish and powerless. I can hear Christians now saying, "Have you been to all the Christian churches in the world, hmmm, have you, *hmmm*?" So, I will preemptively answer. That would be as dumb a question as if I couldn't know what a chocolate chip cookie is because I haven't tried all varieties of chocolate chip cookies around the world. Generally speaking, churches are lousy because they make up THEIR OWN laws, motions and incantations, surreptitiously supplanting God's laws established in the Bible.

As I grew more distant from the church, I didn't outwardly reject God as most who are raised in a "Christian" home do, but I also didn't blindly accept the belief of God because I was told to. I learned to ask a very important word: "Why?" I desperately wanted all religions to be *untrue*. Then I could march to my own drum and make my own rules. I would be free if there were no set rules. If rules were made by people (of which I am one), I could choose which rules to follow or randomly change according to my desires. But to be honest with myself in seeking truth, I had to sincerely check into why I exist. The following pursuit changed my life and my appreciation for God.

Over the past twenty years or so, I was encouraged by *non-Christians* to write a book. I was confused at first why non-Christians would want me to write a book about a "God" they did not believe in, so I laughed it off. I had zero desire to write a book. Ideally, I'd much rather be creating humorous cartoons with my bud Eric than writing this invective of my fellow believers. However, I witnessed too many innocent bystanders being hurt and chased from God by unloving, judgmental, hypocritical Christians that I decided I could no longer bury my head.

The din of the non-Christians exhorting me to write this book grew louder; I began to realize that non-Christians were not so much upset at the idea of God as they were with the people that claimed to represent Him. I heard hundreds of personal stories and saw through non-Christians' eyes the pain that Christians had caused them. So the title, "God is Great but His People Suck" was born.

Christians claim to believe God's "rule book", but often instead of holding themselves to it, they judge the rest of the world by it. This is the exact OPPOSITE of what God asks Christians to do. In 1 Corinthians 5:12 God warns, *"What business is it of mine to judge those outside the church? Are you not to judge those inside? God will judge those outside."* Most non-believing people do not follow and live by the rule book because they do not acknowledge the Author of the rule book. How can Christians hold non-Christians to something they don't believe in? This would be comparable to handing someone on the street the complete NFL rule book and telling them to abide by it. Their first reaction may be, "But I don't play in the NFL!" Christians cannot hold non-Christians to the same standards of God if they aren't on His team. Instead of lasering in on people's sin, Christians need to see the beauty in people and focus on what is most important to God: Love (1 Corinthians 13). Always. In patience and kindness. Even when someone's behavior is contrary to the Word of God or if they are aggressive towards you.

Not tolerance.

Not condoning.

Not accepting. But loving the *person*, not their behavior, action or life choices. Instead of loving their neighbors as themselves, which is what God asks Christians to do, (Mark 12:31), they arbitrarily judge their neighbors by their own standards and traditions. Christians say they know the truth, but their display of it is often embarrassing. No, this is not a blanket indictment for all Christians, all the time. However, I have heard from thousands of non-Christians over three decades why they hate Christians and reject their God. Often the reasons come back to having been judged by Christians or held to standards that they don't claim to believe in.

This is a book of rebuke to the common Christian, (Luke 17:3-4, 1 Timothy 5:20, 2 Timothy 3:16-17, and 4:2). And, "No," I don't think I am Jesus or sinless, which is a common, SENSELESS response leveled at me by Christians when they feel attacked or threatened as I challenge them. In fact, I believe there are many intellectual and compassionate Christians who delve deeper into God's Word than I ever could, making me look like Tiny Tim blithely singing, "Tiptoe through the tulips", while strumming on my toy ukulele. But all Christians are required to rebuke each other in love so we can better each other.

If you don't know the words in the sub-title please look them up. "A polemical look at life with a propitious twist. Written by a pleb." It will give a glimpse into the direction of the book. If you do know the words, you are a word whiz and you deserve a congratulatory virtual chocolate fudge sundae with sprinkles and a cherry on top. I've always liked words, but my father-in-law and William F. Buckley Jr. taught me to love them.

"Suck." Why choose the word "suck" for the title? I suspected by using this word I would be ostracizing myself from Christian publishers, distributors, bookstores… but… meh... So "suck"- what does it even mean? Is the use of the word a sin? Based on the grumblings of a very few Christians, I spent hours talking to hundreds of people seeking a replacement for the word. More than ninety-five percent of those shown the title laughed and heartily agreed. In fact, most enthusiastically stated, "I'd read a book with that title!" Not one non-believer was offended by the title, but only just a few Christians. Christians need to seriously consider why hearty laughing at the title is the typical response. This is one of several reasons for the undertaking of this book.

If you think the word "suck" is harsh, I ask W.D.J.S.- What Did Jesus Say? His words were so harsh and offensive to the elite religious men of his day that they sought to- and eventually did- KILL HIM. Read for yourself the words from Jesus: Matthew 23:13-35:

- *13 "But woe to you, scribes and Pharisees, hypocrites! For you shut the kingdom of heaven in people's faces....*

- *15 Woe to you, scribes and Pharisees, hypocrites! For you travel across sea and land to make a single convert, and when he becomes a convert, you make him twice as much a child of hell as yourselves.*

- *16 Woe to you, blind guides....*

- *17 You blind fools! ...*

- *19 You blind men!...*

- *23 Woe to you, scribes and Pharisees, hypocrites!...*

- *24 You blind guides, straining out a gnat and swallowing a camel!*

- *25 Woe to you, scribes and Pharisees, hypocrites! For you clean the outside of the cup and the plate, but inside they are full of greed and self-indulgence.*

- *26 You blind Pharisee! First clean the inside of the cup and the plate, that the outside also may be clean.*

- *27 Woe to you, scribes and Pharisees, hypocrites! For you are like whitewashed tombs, which outwardly appear beautiful, but within are full of dead people's bones and all uncleanness.*

- *28 So you also outwardly appear righteous to others, but within you are full of hypocrisy and lawlessness.*

- *29 Woe to you, scribes and Pharisees, hypocrites!...*

- *31 ...you witness against yourselves that you are sons of those who murdered the prophets.*

- *33 You serpents, you brood of vipers, how are you to escape being sentenced to hell?"*

As Jesus confronted the religious hierarchy, so am I in this book. Compared to his words, the word "suck" sounds a bit tame now, doesn't it? Would Christians be okay with the title being, "God is Great but His People are Snakes"? or "...His People are Lawless Hypocrites"? What is the difference between "they suck" and calling someone a sinner or a snake or viper or dead man's bones or blind fools or...? And, as stated, Jesus was referring to the religious leaders of his time. Is it any different today? Non-Christians would strongly answer, "No." I have heard hundreds of times from non-Christians the same words Jesus spoke describing today's Christians and leaders: hypocrites, blind, fools, full of greed and self-indulgence. Verse twenty-eight is especially resonant with non-Christians.

Christians, if the above verses are not enough to show that harsh words are often needed, then read on. There are plenty more from Jesus' own lips: Matthew 10:32-36, 12:34, 12:48, 13:15, 13:42, 16:8, 16:23, 17:17. In fact Jesus was so offensive, he was called a glutton, drunkard and a buddy of tax collectors and sinners, (Matthew 11:19.)

Christians, if you say, "Well that's not me. I don't suck," I beg of you to reconsider and read the remainder of this book. God puts us through many trials to refine us into pure gold. The intent of this book is to challenge, sharpen, grow, and love our neighbors better, (Mark 12:30-31, 1 Corinthians 13:4-8).

By simply expressing my opinion and using an occasional "offensive" word, I expect to catch hell from "heavenly" representatives. To which I ask, "Are you perfect"? No? Then this book is for you...for us all:

- This book is for those of you who are doubting your faith. To convince and restore your love of God.

- This book is for the one who is so easily offended by a word and will never reach the people that Jesus hung out with. While you focus on silly words, God focuses on hearts and lives.

- This book is for the fence sitters; perhaps for those who want to believe but can't answer some troubling questions they have about God, or conversely, for those who don't really want to believe but see too much evidence of a Creator.

- This book is for the non-Christian to show you that if Christians were properly doing their God-stated jobs, you would not be so offended and reconsider the true God.

- This book is even for those who agree with the content to encourage and build you up.

- This book is for the "scientist" in all of us because God created and set in motion everything that scientists now study.

I will not say everything correctly in this book and I reserve the right to be wrong. There will be things I wish I didn't put in and there will be things I will slap myself on the forehead for leaving out. I know people will try to pick this book apart, but once you find something you dislike, don't disregard the basic tenets and truths that are being stated here so you won't have to deal directly with your sucky life. Those of you who do this are basically saying, "My life sucks and I'm content with that because it's too hard to think or, *gasp*, consider changing."

2

Who Am I and Who Cares What I Think?

Much of the time in life I feel like an appendix… You exist but you're not sure what for and feel you can be snipped out without anyone noticing. So, ultimately, who am I and who cares what I think since I'm one of seven billion people? These are my opinions based on observations and life experiences. Here is a quick synopsis and some pivotal moments that brought me to the writing of this book, despite NOT wanting to.

I grew up shy and introspective in a home with a loving mother and intellectual father. In retrospect, my upbringing was unremarkable, but I used to think it was bad. I grew up with a brother and sister both smarter than me, but I think I had the edge on wisdom. My parents raised us as best they could, but since they had never been married before and never had experience with birthing and raising kids, we were all guinea pigs. And just like guinea pigs in a cage, squabbles happen, which when you are in them look insurmountable, but when you look back, seem petty. My mom, all 4'10" of her, was the glue that kept the family moving in a positive direction as she introduced life to us, while my dad provided to make that happen. My mom liked church and my dad was initially shoulder-shruggingly agreeable. We regularly attended church and participated in its various activities. I was always wondering what church was really for. Initially I didn't care because many loving families were there and their kids became my friends. In fact forty-five-plus years later, I am finishing this book at one of those friend's house. Typing this, I cannot be more grateful for the outpouring of love Dave and Sandy and his family have shown me. I still have many devoted friends from my upbringing; people I passionately love. For this aspect of the church I am extremely grateful.

Around age fourteen, things changed. I remember standing in church, then sitting, then standing, then sitting, then standing, and reciting stuff we had said every week for years. I guess on this day I snapped. To reiterate from chapter one, when I heard the monotony of the incantations and their robotic deliverance, it woke me to how bored I was and how boring everything around me seemed. I quickly started thinking church and religion may be a charade. At that moment I thought, "God is either true, or a lie and I'm going to find out."

Again, in the Bible, God says to seek Him and you will find Him. But seek Him how, or where? What do you do, whistle "Twee twee," and say, "Here God, God, God…come here God"? Fortunately no - He's "hiding" in *plain sight*. Unbeknownst to me, the journey of finding God had already started…from the day I was born. In Ecclesiastes 3:11 it says, *"He has made everything beautiful in its time. Also, He has put eternity into man's heart, yet so that he cannot find out what God has done from the beginning to the end."* I find this verse interesting. In the first part, it says that everyone has the sense of God and His eternal nature calling us, while the second part seems to say we can't find Him. However, upon closer inspection of the second part, it really says we can't know all that God has done- from the beginning to the end. I take that as it's too grand, too much awesomeness. However in the first part of that verse, I think, even people who deny God still have that smoldering sense within them that He does exist. As much as they try to douse the smoldering, they can't. I too had the sense of God's eternal nature within me, but I thought it was perhaps something that got stuck there from my upbringing in the church. Without much more evidence, my belief in a God was sketchy.

This early chapter of my life also calls to mind an activity my mom did. She drew a squiggly line on a big piece of paper and said to turn the line into a complete drawing. I turned mine into a boxer dog who was boxing. I thought that was clever and so did my mom. She mentioned something about it being inventive and creative. It stuck. I was going to be an inventor and creator. So I thought it was likely I could take the same approach in searching for God.

As I said, growing up was *un*remarkable…or was it? I remember starting to get a reputation for being a rebel. It was NOT because I drank alcohol excessively, took drugs, slept around, lied, cheated, got into angry fights, etc., but because I DIDN'T do those things. That's what most others were doing. A rebel is one who goes against the grain, so if most were messing up their lives, then to *not* do that was being a rebel. I still think it is ironic today when a person has lived a life of abusing themselves and they think they are being a rebel. No, you're not, you're like everyone else! I wanted to be a real rebel and pursue good. Plus I had no desire to upset an understanding and truly loving mother. Why would I want to embarrass her? Why would I want to sully her reputation? So I unintentionally "attacked" the church. In almost every Bible study I have been a part of, I have upset people. I was the guy testing the unbiblical nonsense that people kept saying. Usually it was just their opinion. There is either truth or not, but I wasn't about to accept their made up "truth." Thankfully, throughout my early life and even now, I had core friends who were willing to stay up late with me to discuss the possibility of a real truth.

I went to high school but it didn't take. I was no good at it and hated being there. My dad wanted me to go to college, so I asked the guidance counselor about going to college. He all but laughed out loud. "I don't think it is for you," he said. So I went to college. Whenever someone told me I couldn't, I would, as long as it was "good." I did as well in college as in high school…not well. But all the while, I was still learning, just not the subjects that I was graded on. My approach to college was poor. I didn't want to go, but my dad all but insisted. So I asked how far away I could move and he said it didn't matter. First I looked at schools in Hawaii and Alaska, but there was always something preventing me from going. I had no idea where to go so I looked through a gigantic book called *Barron's Profiles of American Colleges*. I ended up at a tiny school in Waverly, Iowa called Wartburg College. I just read this account to Dave, the friend whose home I am at to finish this book. He said, "Don't you remember how you picked Wartburg?" I said, "No". He said, "You started in the back of the book and worked backwards until you came to the name "Wartburg" and apparently said, "What kind of a name for a school is that!? I'll go there." He was with me when I said this and even though I don't recall that, it sounds like something I would say and do. However, making this haphazard decision was a pivotal moment in my life. One of my best buddies asked if I was nervous going so far away to the middle of a cornfield, knowing no one. I distinctly remember my words to him. They even caught me off guard. I said, "I have friends there I haven't met yet." I was right. My parents drove me to the middle of a cornfield, found the school, and met my roommate Mark. What a fortuitous pairing that was for me. Mark was everything you wanted in a roommate. He was polite, kind, fun, athletic, came from great parents, and would laugh at my antics. By this time my shyness was gone- I thought people who believe in God shouldn't be shy, so I eliminated it from my life. And when I did, I became a bit nutty and would do off-the-cuff stuff. I have since enjoyed the rougher aspects of life but remain a rebel living WITHIN God's guidelines.

I spent two years at Wartburg until they eliminated my program. I loved everything about my experience. The people in Iowa are earthy in the figurative and literal sense. If I told of all my praises for my experience in Iowa, it would fill another book... So I won't. I think the thing most intriguing to me was my roommate who was employing God's love...authentic love. He was patient and kind and he did NOT believe in God. Well, here is proof then that God is not needed. If a kid can turn out so loving without God, why is there a need for God? It was a pivotal moment for me to dig deeper, (so I dug.) While at Wartburg, I was still reading the Bible to see if I could find loopholes and contradictions. I found plenty (or so I thought), but instead of saying, "See this disproves God," I wondered if there was a logical explanation. Even if I couldn't think of one at that moment, I wondered if it was possible that I could think of one at a later time. In time I have found answers to these seeming contradictions. Sometimes the answers come decades later as I learn new facts. Here's an analogy- If I know the basics about car engines but don't know what ALL the parts do, I don't conclude that cars don't exist. It takes time and knowledge to figure out what all the parts are and how they interrelate... so it is with God. We can't know *all* about God right away. It takes time, knowledge and patience to keep digging and seeking Him. He promises that if we keep seeking Him, we will find Him. Never give up searching for the truth...eventually you will find *Him*.

During this time at Wartburg, I read the book of Job. When I got to the end, I got so angry that I threw my Bible across the room because of what I *perceived* as a dumb contest between God and Satan with Job being the stooge stuck in the middle. I was so put off by this test of Job, I said if I couldn't get answers, I would logically use this as evidence for a *disproof* of God. I prayed that the next time I read the book I would understand God's message. I had forgotten I prayed that until the next time I read Job about a year later. This time I matter-of-factly said, "Oh now I understand." I saw that Job was the example for the rest of the world in how to trust and respond to God no matter what suckiness happens in our lives. It also establishes our relationship, in that He is the

Creator and we, the created. Then I remembered my prayer and thanked God deeply for His direct answer to a prayer I initially forgot I prayed. This gave me confidence that God is willing to answer prayers and help our perspectives even when there doesn't seem to be a fair or logical answer.

Since my program no longer existed at Wartburg, I transferred to Kent State in Ohio. Academically, I did as poorly there as I did in all my schooling but continued to learn about life. I met my wife Natalie there. She was beautiful (and still is). I had always found Wonder Woman attractive and that is who I thought Natalie looked like. I could fill (and maybe will) another book of our life. It was difficult. We have five awesome kids. The struggles were the same as my explanation of my upbringing. We were guinea pigs raising five guinea piglets.

I have amazing friends from Kent as well. In fact while I am typing this, my roommate from there, Eric, just texted me and said "Write!" I asked him to hound me to finish this book. He knows me very well. I go gung-ho on a project and then I fizzle. It's been the story of my life that I am ashamed of. Eric is my great friend and cartoon buddy, a complicated person with a solid core, creatively funny and artistically talented. I remember one morning when I went to pour a bowl of my then favorite cereal, Lucky Charms, no cereal came out. I knew I had plenty left so I looked inside the box and saw a colored pencil sketch that Eric drew of Lucky gagged with his hands tied behind his back and a phrase something like, "Oh my stars, faith and begorrah, someone has stolen me lucky charms." Eric and I are still in weekly contact and are launching a series of shirts and other stuff called "Life is Harsh" at LifeisHarsh.com.

While at Kent, a graphics design teacher asked the class to make a bunch of frames in order to make quick proportional borders for magazine layouts. I didn't want to carry a bunch of frames around with the rest of my books so I invented a frame device. It was a frame within a frame, etc.

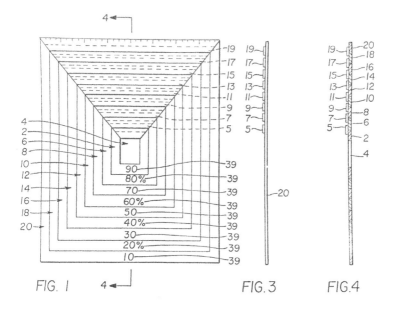

FIG. 1   FIG. 3   FIG.4

I took it out in class, the teacher saw it and asked what it was. I told him and he said, "Put it away, don't show it to anyone and go get it patented." He said if I didn't put it away then I should give it to him and he would get it patented and wouldn't have to work anymore. I thought that was ridiculous but pursued a patent. Eventually I stopped the process because it seemed the patent system was a rigged money grab between the patent attorneys and the patent regulators where I kept paying and they kept delaying, thereby making more money. But that set my inventive mind into high gear. I began coming up with several ideas a day. After a while it became annoying- lots of ideas, nothing to do with them. I started giving ideas away. I remember visiting a friend of mine who lived up the hall one morning. He was a quadriplegic and was using some device to try and remove a disc from his computer. He was having a very difficult time, so I invented a spring-loaded mouthpiece based on the mechanical pencil idea, but with flat grippy ends. Since he didn't have use of his hands, I made it tongue activated so when he pushed the end with his tongue the spring and hands opened and when he let go with his tongue it would close on and grip the disk to pull it out by moving his head backward. He was studying to be a lawyer. He said the design was awesome and he was going to patent it and give me royalties. I never heard from him again.

At the same time, Eric and I were producing a popular cartoon for the campus paper. I came up with the ideas and Eric drew them. I knew I had reached the pinnacle of life when I saw our cartoon cut out of the paper and taped onto a science professor's door. (*See comic strip on opposite page.) I challenged myself to see how many cartoon ideas I could come up with in a day. I came up with fifty and then stopped because I was getting tired thinking of them.

All these inventive ideas and cartoons helped me hone my skills in thinking about life in general, and God by extension. All the time I should have used to study my graded subjects I spent studying other religions, the Bible, history, science, people, relationships, archeology, atheists' beliefs, etc. (No wonder I did so poorly in school.) In order to have a clearer understanding of God you have to pursue Him from many intellectual and experiential ways. Be creative in looking for proof or disproof of Him. Don't reject Him for simple reasons. He made your mind to explore life, and if God truly did create all, then your imaginative mind should uncover His creation as long as your search is truthful rather than agenda driven. Be patient as well. Don't expect to understand if there is a God and who He is quickly. A belief in Him *can* happen right away, but often takes pursuing Him. Pursue Him with your heart, MIND, soul, and strength. Don't quit by listening only to the

world's drivel. How suitably is the world functioning with its humanistic "reasoning"?

After leaving college, Natalie and I married. We had a difficult time over the many years, but this is where the rubber meets the road. Are you going to veer off course or persevere for the long haul as you promised each other? This is where love was put to the test. Through this painful marriage process, it's where I learned love wasn't a feeling but was an action, (as discussed in the next chapter). Similar to patiently pursuing God over time, we are to do that with each other. But, with many couples, rather than "live and learn" from each other, we bail when it doesn't go our way- just like we do to God.

Bailing on God is easy. Just ignore Him and do things your own way. However, by this time, I was convinced that Jesus lived exactly as he said he did and God raised him from the grave, (Romans 10:9). When you get to this point, God will test you in a worthy pursuit towards perfection. So, God tested me, and tested, and tested, until I said, "Okay God, enough testing please. As you can see from my college transcripts I'm not very good at it!" But He *kept* testing.

God tested me in marriage, 5 children, "morality", and business. Early in my married life and career I was trying to turn my inventive, cartoony talents into money. My mother-in-law is a helper and a doer. She set up a meeting with a man from her church called a creative consultant. I had a portfolio filled with ideas. He looked at it and said, "You're going to fail in life." It may not have been that dramatic, but that's what I heard. He said I had *too* many ideas and needed to concentrate on one. This was a setback. I stopped creating so much and poured myself into helping my father at his coin shop, but I was becoming bitter.

A funny song by Buck Owens and Roy Clark from Hee-Haw says, "Gloom, despair, and agony on me. Deep, dark depression, excessive misery. If it weren't for bad luck, I'd have no luck at all.

Gloom, despair and agony on me." Even though I haven't experienced deep dark depression or excessive misery, I still consider life generally difficult. At some points, arduous. At one such point, I stared death in the face when I contracted a disease that kills three out of every five people that get it. I spent time in the hospital as my condition puzzled the doctors. My wife thought I was going to die. I didn't and God didn't. As Monty Python puts it, "I'm not dead yet!" God spared me that time, perhaps to write this book or perhaps He didn't want me annoying people in heaven yet. But even if He didn't spare me, a rock could have just as easily written this book, (Matthew 3:9, Luke 19:40).

Though I consider life generally difficult, often I just need a healthy dose of perspective. Let's look back at the poor schlub, Job; He lost everything precious to him. He was tortured. In fact his plight was so excruciating that the only thing the devil wasn't allowed to do to him was to kill him. Job's good friends came to visit him and didn't even recognize him because he was so disfigured, (Job 2:11-13). I can just picture it now with them walking up to Job and calling for him:

> "JOB?", and they hear,
> "Mmphrgll"........
> **"JOB!?"**..........
> "MRMMFRGLPLL".
> "Job where are you?"

And Job manages to croak out, "Sitting at your feet in these ashes." His friends were so shocked, they wept out loud for him, tore their clothes, and threw ash on their own faces to empathize with his plight. They were so sickened that not one of them knew what to say and just sat with him for a week, both day and night.

Or consider also the apostle Paul's life in 2 Corinthians 11:23-29 where he describes a few of his daily struggles:

... [I] am talking like a madman—with far greater labors, far more imprisonments, with countless beatings, and often near death. Five times I received at the hands of the Jews the forty lashes less one. Three times I was beaten with rods. Once I was stoned. Three times I was shipwrecked; a night and a day I was adrift at sea; on frequent journeys, in danger from rivers, danger from robbers, danger from my own people, danger from
Gentiles,
danger in the city, danger in the wilderness, danger at sea, danger from false brothers; in toil and hardship, through many a sleepless night, in hunger and thirst, often without food, in cold and exposure. And, apart from other things, there is the daily pressure on me of my anxiety for all the churches. Who is weak, and I am not weak?

Compared to these faithful stalwarts my life has not been as comparatively tough, but it doesn't mean it isn't difficult. With Job and Paul as my example, I can better see how to positively deal with life when it throws the inevitable curveball. This gives me a proper perspective and appreciation on what other people have had to endure and how they respond to it. I can learn from them and their difficulties so I don't put myself through the same problems. I'm intrigued by people's manners, words, actions, responses, looks... I hate to admit it, but generally I don't like them. I have sympathy for children, the disabled and the elderly. Everyone else needs to "buck up" by addressing their childhood and conquering their woes. Stop making excuses for yourselves and blaming others, because there are some people who can't do anything about their predicaments. We all need to improve and do what God suggests. Whether you believe in God or not, my guess is you need to change many aspects of your life. Right now I'm sure we all can think of many things that we need to change, or stop doing, or start doing to improve our lives. So I implore you to *start* today and ask others to help when you falter.

Although I don't like people, I have come to enjoy truthful quests with them. I'm continuing to learn by listening and asking questions. It's curious to learn how people have become who they are by how they've lived, and it's usually through pain. Part of my learning how to understand people was playing chess against a computer. At first when I played the computer, it destroyed me even on the simplest level. I couldn't understand how I could lose so consistently… until I studied what the computer was doing to me. It was constantly attacking and I was defending. You can't win by just defending with no offense. So then when the computer would put me in a sticky situation, I looked to put it in a worse one. The computer then started defending its pieces, presenting me with an opportunity to go on the offensive. I rose quickly through the levels to a point where I needed to be more of a student of the game to advance further. I applied aspects of chess into dealing with people. Usually when unbelievers condescendingly attack Christians they do it on numerous fronts. Often the very questions they are "asking", they have not resolved in their own lives. So start asking them similar difficult questions. Put them on the defensive, but do it without the snarkiness with which they typically employ. When they are forced to answer difficult life questions, you'll find out they don't have all the answers either. Now the playing field is level and you can start in real and meaningful dialog.

In my experience, most people talk with bluster and little facts, but screech and squawk in an authoritative way that it makes them sound knowledgeable. I have come to be aware that most people, including myself, have shallow knowledge. In fact I don't think it is even wise to call people *smart*. We are all ignorant. Even the "smartest" people are pitifully imbecilic compared with the unfathomable complexities of

God's creation. Rather than say someone is smarter than another, we should actually say they are slightly less ignorant! Robert Frost said something akin to, "We all proceed on insufficient knowledge." So if you criticize my opinion in this book, do you really know any better? This is an opinion book based on experience, education, and a study of life, culminating in the belief that God's Word is important, but mine?...not so much.

There is an infinite amount of learning that we can do on almost any subject; for instance, study the brain- we still don't know most of its capabilities even though we've been studying it for centuries now... this is the beauty of God and His Word. It's like chemistry- you can know the basics and just live, or you can study for the rest of your life and never get close to the depths of what it has to offer. We are still adding new elements to the periodic chart and don't know how many are yet to be discovered; the ultimate result of this should be humility, seeing the depth of what we *don't* know even after spending a lifetime learning.

I have also learned from people who would consider what I believe to be ignorant or even dangerous. I like quality thinkers regardless of whether they agree with me. One of my favorites was Christopher Hitchens. I called him the Christian Slayer. He was the Colosseum where Christians met their doom. Even though I believed his life conclusions were wrong, I would love watching his masterful, wit-filled way of first disarming his opponents and then going in for the intellectual kill. Was there no Christian gladiator that could defeat this foe? I began training to take him on if I could ever have the honor. In all likelihood, I too would be mauled, but, I thought, if I had the right equipment, I might eventually learn to defeat him. I listened to hundreds of hours of him, learning to defend and hone my beliefs. But along came a roly-poly, elderly man that reminds me of a grown up, marshmallow-looking, Pop-n-Fresh doughboy. The new gladiator's name was John Lennox from Oxford, England. I thought, "Eww this is going to be messy... pop-n-fresh against a vicious tiger." The tiger savagely attacked using his first twenty minutes to launch his brutal verbal assault. I looked away in dismay that another Christian was about to be devoured by this secular humanist tiger. Pop-n-Fresh sauntered to the lectern appearing unfazed by the salvo and launched a counter attack that wounded the tiger. You could see it on the tiger's face. "He's wounded!" "THE TIGER IS WOUNDED!" The fight went on for nearly two hours, but when the dust settled, Doughboy stood over the vanquished tiger. Hitchens even admitted defeat and asked for a rematch. Lennox won in the best way possible; with intelligence, wisdom, humor, humbleness, and, best of all, an appreciation for his opponent, dealing with him in love, and complimenting him while disagreeing with him.

I loved listening to Hitchens, but unfortunately his voice fell silent when he died of cancer. However there are plenty of other outspoken Christian skeptics to take his place like Sam Harris, Penn Jillette, and Joe Rogan, to name a few. But there are also Christian thinkers that are formidable and could defeat any nonreligious person in a debate, such as Ravi Zacharias and his entire RZIM team (which includes John Lennox), David Wood, Nabeel Qureshi (whose voice remorsefully also fell silent), Lee Strobel, Frank Turek, and numerous others.

As long as I breathe, I continue to learn from all sides. Again, my life has been one of listening, studying and talking. I'm not a big fan of going to the mall to shop, but I love going there to listen to and marvel at the theater of life being performed on a daily basis. It's like a circus parade of misfits, one in which I fit right in- you don't even have to pay to see this circus and they let anyone join in the parade! There's the storky tall, always looking a bit gaunt because of the atmospheric air he breaths, and the teeny tiny. And over there is the egghead, where you wouldn't want to ask him what time it was because you would end up at the wrong end of a lecture of quantum physics. He's holding hands with "the pear," whose head is normal sized, but her butt is so huge you feel like decorating her at Christmas. There's the very old, but on close inspection you realize it's a meth-head, and the way-too-young, making you wonder where the hell their parents are. There's the rich, who are so vain their plastic surgery makes them look like a store mannequin, and the poor, who although you haven't seen them yet, you know they're around because somethin' smells funny. And look- there's Mr. Studly who has a serious case of the "gap syndrome"... you know... where he holds his arms out to the side of his body pretending he is more muscular than he actually is. He's being intimidated by some puffed-up, punk-ass kid trying to overcompensate for being a short s***.

The misfit parade keeps coming. I join them so other mall-watchers can laugh at me. Go ahead and laugh, it's all a part of a harsh world that I understand and embrace. I walk among the lonely, the boisterously overconfident, the extrovert and the introvert, the sporty and slobs... I hear their meaningless "weather talk," sometimes thoughtful observations, and the "don't care 'bout nuffin" sentiments. Some love to hear themselves talk, while others obsessively take selfies. But it just keeps going... there is the beautiful on the outside, but ugly on the inside, versus the ugly on the outside but beauty within. These people are just a small representation of the whole world.

The list of personal traits and characteristics never ends. Everyone needs to embrace who they are and change what they can, if possible. Sometimes life deals a harsher hand, but we still need to laugh at and enjoy ourselves, and love others. Please do an internet search for Nick Vujicic and Lizzie Velasquez. If anyone has a right to scream how unfair life is, they would be in the top one percent. Nick was born with no limbs- only part of a foot. Yet he gloriously overcame, and is now married and a joy-filled MOTIVATIONAL speaker. Lizzie likewise majestically overcame a harsh genetic disorder that left her disfigured and blind in one eye. She was harassed as the most ugly woman in the world. Yet she too is a motivational speaker! Two beautiful souls that can inspire you to be all that you can be with *whatever* you have. The more I talk to people, the more I learn about how vastly different we are in some respects, but on the inside we are made up of 99.99 % of the same stuff and we all want the same thing... LOVE.

Learning has been key in my life to defend and live a free life pursuing God's purposes. I don't read my Bible every day, but when I do, I quietly ask God to let me continue to learn about life. Another pivotal moment in my life came one morning when I picked up the Bible held it open up in the air and prayed, asking if God wanted me to read something specific. Normally, I get no response. This is not because God is not involved, as the naysayers would taunt, but because God wants us to be adults and figure out life on our own without Him babysitting us every minute of the day. If God does want to let us know something specific, He will. That morning, He did.

I can't adequately express how God communicates, but I know it is through the Holy Spirit whom He promises everyone when they place their trust in Jesus, (Acts 2:38). God sometimes speaks in a still, small voice, (1 Kings 19:11-13). I believe He speaks this way to see if we are listening. That morning I distinctly "heard" the still small voice. God answered my prayer by saying He wanted me to read 1 Corinthians 13:4-8. I laughed out loud because I knew that verse well. Thinking I heard wrong, I spoke back and said, "I already know that verse and could quote it word for word." I immediately "heard" back in a patient "voice," "I didn't ask you if you could quote it, I just simply asked if you would *read* it." I heard this as clearly as if I were talking to a friend. I was completely confused. Why would God ask me to read something I already knew *verbatim*? I was still doubting, but I read the verses...

> *"Love is patient and kind; love is not jealous or boastful; it is not arrogant or rude. Love does not insist on its own way; it is*

not irritable or resentful; it does not rejoice at wrong, but
rejoices in the right. Love bears all things, believes all things,
hopes all things, endures all things. Love never ends,"

...it was as if I had never read the verses before. The world became brighter...fabulously free. I felt joy and shame. I had known God's definition of love and tried to employ it throughout my life, but on that morning God gave me fresh eyes to read it. I apologized for laughing at God and thanked Him for the message. I said to Him, "So this is my job as a Christian, to love people." And He simply replied, "Yep." Not the formal, "Yes," as if that would make Him more Godly; He was speaking to me, and knew I would hear "yep" as an endearing response. And I *did* think it was very cool. "Yep" and nothing more. God knew I understood and didn't need to say anything else.

I employed my renewed understanding of God's love to all my customers, family, friends, and acquaintances. It gave me a heart for the hurting, to talk about life and see what we can do to improve it and help each other. I remember shortly after this revelation a guy that was blitzed out of his mind staggered into our store. I mean, he was bumping into both walls of the store as if he were a dinghy in a raging sea. He slurred several incoherent words. I don't know why he came in and I doubt he knew either. Then he left the same way he came in… bump, bump, bump...out the door. Rather than condemning and slandering him, I thought, "I wonder if that's how I look to God sometimes… stumbling about, thinking and speaking incoherent gibberish."

Not everyone needs a "love revelation" to love well. My mother displayed love well. So, in wrapping up this chapter, I will bring it back to me as the 14- year- old where I started to question everything. At the point where I was questioning the validity of God, I said to my mom, "I'd rather be a hippie than a Christian." She didn't flip out, she just patiently asked, "Why?" I said, "Because I believe hippies are really searching for the truth and Christians are just pretending." Peace and love, man, that's what the hippies tried to reach and I deeply respected that goal. I later came to realize that their goal was completely right and biblical, but they left out the key component... the Creator of that peace and love. Keeping God in mind, I consider myself a hippie at heart. And whenever I go into those happy thoughts, for some reason, Blind Melon's song, *No Rain*, plays in my brain.

Shortly after my love revelation, my gem of a mother was diagnosed with pancreatic cancer. It's a death sentence, usually within months. This news was a hammer-fist to the gut. I am, however, completely aware of the realities of life- it eventually leads to death- sometimes in the most horrific of ways. My mother had an operation, contracted sepsis, went unconscious and was being kept alive by people, machines, tubes, and drugs. She shrunk to sixty pounds. I lost hope but my brother and sister did not. My mom pulled a Monty Python just like I had years earlier and said, "I'm not dead yet." She survived an amazing five more years. When she died, we were all with her.

We all loved my mom deeply, but there were few tears. There was actually more joy than there were tears. In fact, my brother played a video of a snickers commercial where an old guy is in line being interviewed for heaven. It was hilarious and we all busted out laughing. We had to explain to the nurses outside the door that we were not sick bastards, but we could laugh even in a moment like this because we knew my mom entered into bliss. In an instant she went from old, sick and frail, to a new body with no more pain, sorrow or tears, (Revelations 21:4). The day after my mom died, my niece wrote on the back window of her car, "Our grandma was born YESTERDAY!" I bet my mom is saying to me now, "I look forward to when you get here so I can show you around." I never think of her as dead, but living blissfully and having the time of her "life." Every time I think of her, I smile.

Frank Sinatra crooned, "Regrets I have a few, but then again too few to mention." Well Frank is a better person than I, because my life is full of regrets. This doesn't mean every day I wake up and say, "Woe is me," and hit myself in the head with a board like Monty Python's monks. It just means I would like a mulligan, and amazingly, that is what God affords me… and everyone else. The mulligan is God's forgiveness no matter what you have done.

This chapter has been about a few key, pivotal moments that changed the course of my life, but if I'm honest, my entire life is a contiguous "pivotal moment." Every step, every decision, every person I have met, my lifelong friends, got me to where I am now, whether good or bad. Since I have come to believe in Jesus, I want to continually work towards being more like Him. As a result of professing this belief, I will be judged more harshly, (James 3:1). It is fair. I will strive to improve, and have a long way to go. Eventually, I want to get to the point that when I die and meet my Maker, He will simply say, "Well done Brad."

3

LOVE

Love. Love changed my life.

But what is it, and who defines it?

Tina Turner sang: "What is love but a second- hand emotion?"[1]

Shakespeare: "Love looks not with the eyes, but with the mind." *(A Midsummer's Night Dream)*[2]

Fyodor Dostoevsky: "What is hell? I maintain that it is the suffering of being unable to love." *(The Brothers Karamazov)*[3]

C.S. Lewis: "To love at all is to be vulnerable. Love anything and your heart will certainly be wrung and possibly broken." *(The Four Loves)*[4]

Richard Dawkins said in a letter to his ten- year- old daughter, "There are outside things to back up the inside feeling: looks in the eye, tender notes in the voice, little favors and Kindnesses."[5]

Or how about this deep lyrical gem by P!nk in a song called "True Love"[6]:

Sometimes I hate every single stupid word you say
Sometimes I wanna slap you in your whole face
At the same time, I wanna hug you
I wanna wrap my hands around your neck
You're an asshole but I love you
But I hate you, I really hate you,
So much, I think it must be
True love, true love

My daughter Alexandra did a study and asked twenty Christians and twenty non-Christians what love is. It was eye-opening to see that Christians and non-Christians answered remarkably similarly. Here are some of their answers:

- the more one judges the less one loves
- love isn't real, it's a made-up human emotion
- love is not explainable
- you know it when you have it

Merriam-Webster defines it as "a feeling of strong or constant affection for a person: attraction that includes sexual desire."

The more I looked at the vast dissimilarity in the definitions of love, the clearer it became that the world defines it based on the circumstantial feelings. It took me most of my life to understand the true definition of this word. And it will take the remainder of my life to *practice* it. As I stated before, I grew up churchized so I knew the word love because it is succinctly defined in the Bible. I even accepted the definition because it made sense to me. 1 Corinthians 13:4-8 is on many homes' walls and is in most weddings. In fact, the biblical definition is so well known that I think it has become trite and overlooked. It is just something to recite at weddings for bobbleheaded Christians to say amen to, shed a tear or two… and then promptly forget. When something becomes trite, it is then vulnerable to reinterpretation.

This may initially sound ridiculous, but the greatest offense to God is to not love. "But," you say, "What about murder, hurting children, etcetera?" Think about it, if you were to truly love God's way, would there be anyone that would even think about doing such horrific things? "Crimes" are committed against God, (sin), BECAUSE people DO NOT LOVE! And crimes are committed against each other because we do not love by how God defined it. So what is love? As you saw above, love is defined in a myriad of ways, some very fun, some dumb, some thoughtful, but I would argue none so poignant and perfect as God's definition:

> *"Love is patient and kind; love is not jealous or boastful; it is not arrogant or rude. Love does not insist on its own way; it is not irritable or resentful; it does not rejoice at wrong, but rejoices in the right. Love bears all things, believes all things, hopes all things, endures all things. Love never ends,"* (1 Corinthians 13:4-8a).

I'm a stickler for this word. I defend it when Satan tries to change and marginalize it. I've come to believe there is only one foundational definition of love. Any other defined substitute is not love. Sex is not love, it is lovemaking, coitus, copulation… but it is not love. Feelings are not love… they are… well, feelings. Saying "I love you," is a compilation of words, but not love. Love is an ACTION. You must engage in an active role of practicing it.

Here it is broken down into just the main words. Love is:

- Patient
- Kind
- Not arrogant
- Not rude
- Does not insist on its own way
- Not irritable
- Not resentful
- Does not rejoice at wrong
- Rejoices at right
- Bears all
- Believes all
- Hopes all
- Endures all
- Never ends

If we were being honest, how well do we stack up against God's "love" words? Whenever I share this definition of love with people they often cringe when making a mental checklist comparing themselves to these words. Most say they fail horribly on the very first word- patience. I agree. In my observations this is the biggest problem with people. Just think how many of the world's problems would be solved if this single word, "patience," were practiced and employed consistently. Impatient parents are destroying their children. These growing, learning children are actually being shown by their parents how to *hate* because their parents are not employing God's patience. And that is just the first word. Look at the other words and see how you personally stack up. I bet you **struggle** on several of the words and if you think that you don't, ask your family and friends which ones you **fail** at. I bet their answer would be humbling.

"Luvya." I hear this said flippantly and vapidly. At least Shakespeare said it with some meaning, "I love you, let me count the ways..." "Luvya" is like many of the other "terms of endearment" that I hear people spout to each other, like, "dear... honey... sweet baboo." Terms of endearment aren't wrong if they are stated with actual genuine meaning, but when I hear people say them, ironically it is usually in the negative sense- such as, "I see you didn't take the trash out again... *HONEY.*" If you say, "I love you" right after you were impatient with that person, your "I love you", is voided by your representation of unlove.

Not only does the world redefine love, but Christians do, too. A preacher in a recent sermon I heard stated the definition of love as, "an act of the will, accompanied by emotion, which results in action on behalf of the one being loved." I may be daft, but he seems to have muddied up what God stated clearly. To be perfectly honest, I don't know what the heck he was saying.

A Christian psychologist/counselor I talked with asked whether I knew what the five love languages were. I responded light-heartedly, "No, and I don't care." I said this because God already gave us a clear definition of love in the Bible and nothing can improve on that. Apparently it is a book that is popular in Christian circles, but I had never heard of it. According to this counselor, the book boiled down to five main love languages:

1) Quality time
2) Words of affirmation
3) Giving of gifts
4) Acts of service
5) Physical touch

Initially, the list looks fine. Ironically, however, the five so-called "love languages" book gets it nearly backwards. When talking to this counselor later, I told him I thought it was backwards and I rewrote them. Here is what I think *God's* five love languages are, broken into sections and subsections based on 1 Corinthians 13:4-7:

1) Patience
-not irritable

2) Kindness
-does not insist on its own way
-not resentful

3) Humbleness
-not jealous
-not boastful
-not arrogant
-not rude

4) Rejoices at right

5) Hope that never ends
-bears all
-believes all
-hopes all
-endures all

If God's five love languages were followed, then the other "five love languages" would be the natural outcome. If someone *was* patient and kind with you, you would naturally want to spend time with that person, say nice things to them, give them gifts, do stuff for them, and of course- be snuggly with them!

If we do not use God's definition of love then whose are we using? PEOPLE'S! That's right, poor schlubs like me and you. Why should we pay any attention to their definition? So if we are going to make up our own definitions, then I like these funnier ones:

- "Love is temporary madness. It erupts like a volcano and then subsides."[7]

  or perhaps the number one definition voted on in Urban Dictionary:

- Love is "nature's way of tricking people into reproduction."

Because love altered the way I interact with people, I've had numerous people tell me I am in the wrong business, suggesting I should be a counselor. I respond that if I were, I would starve to death. I can image the scenario of a struggling couple coming into my office. They bemoan each other and state their woes. Yap yap yap yap yappity yap. Yappity yap yappity… yap, at which point I would respond with one of my favorite Bugs Bunny characters, Mugsy, retorts, "Shaddup, shuttin up! Button yer lip!" After getting their attention, I would say, "One or most likely both of you are violating one or several words of God's definition of love." I would give them the list and tell them to STOP IT- stop insisting on their own way and instead love God's way. (Bob Newhart has a very funny routine on this. Just type his name and "Stop it" into YouTube.) There would be no need for follow-up sessions, so I would starve… and I'm not into that. The Bible says there is wisdom in counsel. So I am not against "counseling", but if the counselors counsel isn't laser focused on God's love, then it is folly.

Relationships would self-correct if you would humble yourself and practice each individual love words in the areas where you are weak. Think about your defective relationships and compare it to the above *Love List*. I'll bet that you will see right away why there is a problem between you and your "antagonist." But rather than do this, it seems like most people are content to be discontented. That's right, discard your husband, wife and/or children. Cheat on each other because you have "irreconcilable differences!" Go on, you DESERVE better. No, it's not YOU that has to change, it's them. "If you only knew the half of what they…blah blah blah." If we were to all do this, we would eventually all be living alone. We all have differences for crying out loud!

I debated with a Christian psychologist about what love was. He told me there were four types of love in the Bible: Agape, Phileo, Storge, and Eros. I didn't know if this was true or not so I studied and uncovered there really are only two, Agape and Phileo. Storge is connected with Phileo. Eros is not in the Bible. So I did an etymology study on the word and found it originally was a mythological Greek god of harsh "love," or some might say rape. I wondered how most Christians have come to believe that this word is biblical. Looking further, I found "eros" dropped out of written lexicon for hundreds of years until none other than Sigmund Freud around 1925 used the word and manipulated it into its current definition. There is "erotic" talk in the Bible, but eros is not defined by God and has no part of the word "love."

I discovered that "love" is used in the King James Bible 310 times. If it is used so often in the Bible, I'm glad God gave a specific definition. So when God has defined love perfectly, why is the world and much more importantly, THE CHURCH redefining it? The world doesn't necessarily embrace God's definition and logically wouldn't abide by it, but Christians should know better. Instead, Christians often set themselves up to be rightly criticized and labeled as hypocrites because they do not abide by God's definition of love.

So let's look at each word of love again: patient and kind; not jealous or boastful; it is not arrogant or rude. Love does not insist on its own way; it is not irritable or resentful; it does not rejoice at wrong, but rejoices in the right. Love bears all things, believes all things, hopes all things, endures all things. Love never ends. Are *any* of these words complicated or confusing? NO! You don't read them and say, "I wonder what those mean." Quite to the contrary, they are refreshingly simple to understand! LOVE is THE answer to all relational problems. If you are having problems with anyone- spouse, kids, boss, dog, whatever- one or both of you is not loving the way God wants.

To see whether this definition of love is precise let's reverse the words and see whether it defines hate well:

Hate is impatient and unkind; hate is jealous and boastful; it is arrogant and rude. Hate insists on its own way; it is irritable and resentful; it rejoices at wrong, but does not rejoice at right. Hate bears nothing, believes nothing, hopes in nothing, and does not endure. Love ends.

Is this a accurate definition of hate? YES!

With a solid definition of love now, let's think about God's greatest commands. First, *"...you shall love the Lord your God with all your heart and with all your soul and with all your mind and with all your strength."* (Mark 12:30-31) So, Love God = Agape love. God expects us to apply His definition to Him first. After all, if there is a God and He made us, then it would make sense to acknowledge Him first. When things don't go our way, are we patient and trusting of Him? Usually we are not and quickly say, "Why me?" Think how annoying this would be to a God who is perfect. "Why me?" This is not a question God appreciates. Job (a man God called innocent), after being tormented by Satan, asked this simple "why me" question. God went on for three chapters (38-40), verse after verse after verse, establishing His holiness to Job:

- *"Were you there when I laid the foundations of the earth?"*
- *"Did you place the stars in the sky?"*
- *"Shall a faultfinder contend with the Almighty?"*
- *"Is it by your wisdom the hawk soars?"*

Job apologized in chapter 42.

God's second greatest command says, *"You shall love your neighbor as yourself."* After Agape love is Phileo love = love your neighbor. Most people will respond positively when you practice God's love, (yes it takes practice, LOTS of practice). But some people will try to take advantage of your kindness by manipulating God's words. An example of that today would be the word "tolerance." The world today says if you aren't tolerant then you aren't loving. Tolerance, however, is NOT a definition of love. Notice how nearly opposite the world's definition of love is versus God's. Love has been changed from an action to a feeling. Today, most people you ask to describe love would list it as an emotion, not the *action* that it is. Anyone can get adept at love because they can practice doing these words. And you know what they say, "Practice makes perfect." If it's just a feeling then love is just whatever anyone… well… feels. Which ultimately means nothing since we all "feel" differently.

Anyone who calls themselves a Christian must overcome any fear or obstacles holding them back from loving God's way and step onto the world's stage to display love correctly. Isaiah 41:10 puts it this way; *"So do not fear, for I am with you; do not be dismayed, for I am your God. I will strengthen you and help you; I will uphold you with my righteous right hand."* If we love appropriately, the world will take note and say, "I want that." Do it poorly and they will say, "No thanks" to God.

Christians, if you are active in studying the Bible, involved in Bible clubs and groups, listen to sermons, attend church regularly, read Christian books, give to charities, do good works, pray your heart out, etc., BUT, you aren't first pursuing God's simple definitions of love then STOP EVERYTHING you are doing. Please read the ominous verses right before where love is defined- 1 Corinthians 13:2 *"...and if I have prophetic powers, and understand all mysteries and all knowledge, and if I have all faith, so as to remove mountains, but have not love, I am nothing."* Even Jesus said he does not know all mysteries, including the end of the age. Only God can match this description. The verses are in effect saying if you are as great as God, but do not love in the way He defines, THEN YOU ARE NOTHING!

Moses was a murderer, (Exodus 2:11-12). He broke the first word in the definition of love by being impatient with God and taking things into his own hands. God said vengeance is His, (Deuteronomy 32:35-36). Later, Moses returned back to Egypt and led the Israelites out into the desert at God's request. But again Moses became impatient and as a consequence, God disallowed him from entering the promised land. In Numbers 20:10-12 God says,

> *"And Moses and Aaron gathered the assembly together before the rock, and he said to them, 'Hear now, you rebels; shall we bring forth water for you out of this rock?' And Moses lifted up his hand and struck the rock with his rod twice; and water came forth abundantly, and the congregation drank, as did their cattle. And the Lord said to Moses and Aaron, 'Because you did not believe in me, to sanctify me in the eyes of the people of Israel, therefore you shall not bring this assembly into the land which I have given them.'"*

Christians, let's stop preaching at people and start loving God's way. Then non-Christians will know we really do care about them and when we listen to them, they in turn may listen to us. But if you try to force your point on people, not only is that being hateful, (insisting on your own way), but you will often drive them further from God. Love the *proper* way and practice, practice, practice. Love will make you WANT to change your life for the better. Implementing love properly will draw others to this truth. I experienced this personally with a customer:

One afternoon, a self- professed lesbian walked into my store with many items to sell. We struck up a conversation about everyday life stuff and began conversing fairly easily. Even though I don't talk about my faith unless it comes up naturally, I must have used a word that may have sounded churchy. I don't know what I said, but it set the conversation in a new direction. She growled, "You're not a Christian are you?" I said, "Does it matter? Who cares what I think." "Because if you are, we are not going to get along," she responded. I answered with a smile, "Well in that case, yes, I am a Christian, and you and I will get along just fine. Not only will we get along, but you're going to like me and…" (kiddingly) "you're going to have to apologize for saying that, after we are done." She **said**, "Never." So I asked her if we could continue with our business and talk and just see how it goes- to which she agreed. We had a fascinating conversation. I straight up asked her (to be funny), what it was like to be a lesbian since I wasn't one. She was like a bull, not only in size and attitude, but because she was constantly trying to shake me off her back by purposefully speaking in a raunchy manner.

She was an intimidating woman. She was, without exaggerating, about twice my weight and had a 1960's sergeant's butch haircut. She described the act of lesbian sex, details of her current sexual relationship, and tried hard to get me to blanch. I didn't. I love people like this. Talk raunchy. I don't care. It's not my job to judge. Plus it opens up gritty, real dialogue by addressing her life. I was thrilled with the conversation and had no idea where it was going. At some point she loosened up her aggression, however the conversation stayed *very* earthy. I can't recall all that was talked about, but I just thought about how much I appreciated the talk. I truly did and she could tell.

Because I listened to her without condemnation, it freed up the conversation to be one that could go two ways. She became willing to hear my thoughts on life. It turned into a wonderful back-and-forth talk. I was able to ask her about her life growing up and if she had any religious experience. That's where she opened up about being abused and taken advantage of. I've heard this numerous times before when talking to people and it makes me clench my teeth and curl my knuckles at the injustice they had to endure. She even asked if I thought homosexuality was wrong. My answer was that since I now completely believe in the God of Jesus, it doesn't matter what I believe, it matters what God said (...and "no" you heathen dissenters, this does not mean I am a mind numbed robot. It means, over decades, I have come to trust my Father in heaven as anyone comes to trust a parent or friend over time through them proving themselves). I asked her (my lesbian friend), whether she wanted me to show her the verses in the Bible that speak to homosexuality, and she said, "No." I was content with this answer since it is all in God's timing and not mine. I think she knew the answer but was not ready to hear God's Word convict her. Nevertheless, I would go on loving her in the manner that my God asks me. We finished our business that day and she said she had more items to sell and would come back again. She did.

I was excited to see her again and said, "Hey Jennifer…" She was surprised, and I could tell, pleased, that I remembered her name. I'm less than proficient in remembering names, but after our gritty conversation, I couldn't forget her. Also, embarrassingly, my presupposition of how a Jennifer was supposed to look didn't match her, as if all Jennifers look the same. Really dumb of me, I know, but I'm just being honest. We did more significant business where she was pleased with my offers and I was pleased with what she was selling. We had another appreciable conversation, but this time she had no edge. It was clear she had accepted me. When we were wrapping things up she made a beautiful gesture of friendship. Jennifer would probably hate me saying this, but she said to me in a non-aggressive, softer voice, "I wanted to tell you that I do like you and I enjoyed our conversations." With uplifting joy in my heart, I laughed and thanked her for this admission and for the conversation, because I too enjoyed it and learned from it. I asked her if she knew why she liked me. She scrunched her face and said "No." She said she even had a conversation with her girlfriend about me and couldn't figure out why she didn't hate me like all other Christians she has come in contact with. She also expressed that the conversation with her girlfriend did not go well. It seemed like her girlfriend was jealous and she did not want Jennifer to see me anymore. I suggested the reason Jennifer liked me was because it isn't my job to judge her, but that it is my first duty to love and truly listen to her. She quietly shook her head in agreement.

I was able to share the verses where Jesus gave that same answer to a man when he asked what the most important commandments were. And Jesus answered that we are to love God and love people first, and then said all the other commandments hang on these two, (Matthew 22:34-40). Nothing is more important. Then Jennifer startled me by saying, "...and I'm sorry." She remembered saying at the start that she and I would never get along. I was kidding when I said she would have to apologize for saying that, but I didn't expect or deserve for her to actually do so, and yet she did anyway. To this day, I wish she would come back in so we could continue our brief friendship. I have not seen her since, but perhaps I will once again when God makes the last call.

But until that last call, we are all stuck here together on this beautiful blue marble. It is true love which will make it a whole lot easier to get along no matter what we believe. God said to Adam that it is not good to be alone. Loneliness is dangerous and depressing. It can be overcome easily with love. If someone doesn't reach out to you in love, then reach out to them. Parents, you are the example of love for your children. They don't need stuff, they need you to *demonstrate* God's love. This starts very early. They watch and listen to your tone and your words. Trying to teach them to be a decent person won't work if you are showing impatience and unkindness, envy, or arrogance. I appreciate Jesus' practical answer to an arrogant snob, when asked about being "good" and making it into heaven, in Luke 10:25-28:

> On one occasion an expert in the law stood up to test Jesus. *"Teacher,"* he asked, *"what must I do to inherit eternal life?" "What is written in the Law?"* he replied. *"How do you read it?"* He answered, *"Love the Lord your God with all your heart and with all your soul and with all your strength and with all your mind"; and, "Love your neighbor as yourself." "You have answered correctly,"* Jesus replied. *"Do this and you will live."*

Take the love challenge. Identify the love words that you need to improve and actively practice being better at them. See if people notice, and *when* they do... repeat. It will set you on a new course and refresh your soul.

4

Gushing Souls

Destroyed lives, deep woe, confusion, theft, addiction, hatred, betrayal, suicide, pain, sorrow, depression, disease, dying children, lies, regret…

…melt into tears, redemption, grace, forgiveness, truth, peace, kindness, respect, joy, laughter, freedom…

In our society there is a phrase that says you don't talk about politics or religion. This is stated because people have lost the art of speaking in love. Discourse on politics and religion often angrily devolves into impatience, unkindness, arrogance, rudeness and insisting on your own way. I never cease to be amazed at how vehemently one will defend a position with scant information and how invective the argument becomes. Spirited arguing is healthy, but do it in love. Listen as much, if not more than, talk. As one customer put it, "That's why we have two ears and one mouth." Since I dance to the tune of a different drummer, I do talk about politics and religion at our business if people want to. Initially members of my family and coworkers were reluctant for me to engage in this banter, but I felt if I wasn't part of real discourse then I was guilty of complicity in the decline of culture. So, a maxim for the store was created: "We want to do good business here, but we DO talk politics and religion and if you don't want to you'll have to leave," as I point towards the door. This is usually received in the fun, loving way it is meant with an occasional shocked look. Most people actually will engage in these subjects in a kind way, which has lead to thousands of wonderful stories and countless moments of humor and tears.

Another phrase that I use occasionally when first timers walk into the store. When they say happily, "How are you doing today?" I flatly respond, "What do you care?" I don't say this all the time, just occasionally to have fun and watch their eye-popping uncomfortable reaction. It's fun to take people out of their comfort zone. They significantly relax when I laugh and tell them I'm kidding.

Humor is critical in so many aspects of life. I love creative comedic thinking, inventing, being an idea guy, and thinking outside the box. But since college I have been helping my father at his business that really is the antithesis of what I enjoy. The beginnings were rough. I graduated from college with a graphic design focus and was ready to tackle the world. My friend Eric and I had a popular cartoon running in the paper for a few years and my "career" looked promising. "Nope," said God, "You're going to help your dad." "Nope," said I... Guess who won?

"Oh yeah, God? If I'm going to be stuck here, then I'm going to fold my arms across my chest, tightly curl my mouth down, gripe and complain." I got good at this... I can see the scenario in heaven right now between my "guardian angel" approaching God and saying, "Brad's really upset with the direction of his life," and God saying something profound like, "So?"

That's right, as the years passed I grew to be unhappy with being at the store. "Why God? Why did you give me seemingly unlimited inventive/creative ideas if I'm not able to effectively use them?" I felt my talents and life were wasting away. I was becoming bitter. I knew it. I could feel it. I hated it. I needed a change- not necessarily of careers, but attitude. I had already had my first daughter (the one that is helping me to write this book now!), and I didn't want my attitude to infect her. My solution was to put a pad of paper and pen next to my bed with the promise that in the morning I would start a list of what was positive about life; to focus on the positive and try to change the negative. Well, I woke up and put pen to paper. The first thing I wrote is, "I woke up." Then the list seemed to take on a life of its own as if God were writing it. "Uh oh," I said. "I don't like where this is going." I spent a total of about 10 minutes on the list and it went something like this:

WHAT IS GOOD ABOUT TODAY:

- I woke up
- Healthy
- In a nice bed
- In a house
- Healthy daughter
- Wife next to me
- Put my feet on the ground to walk
- Breathe without thinking about it
- Friends and family love me

I was feeling guilty and sick of my previous self... I walked to the bathroom to shower. I adjusted the hot and cold to my precise liking, ahhhhh just perfect, until I remembered an image from National Geographic (if I recall correctly) that flashed in my mind of a joyful child showering under a peeing cow. (NOT KIDDING). My hands froze on the shower knobs. I teared up knowing how ungrateful I had been to God and all those not as fortunate as myself. The cow kid was happier than me. I reached out of the shower curtain and angrily tore the list out of the paper pad, crumpled the paper and whipped it into the trash. I cursed at myself and then apologized to God. My life changed that morning.

I still didn't want to be at the store, but from then on I thanked God every day for His providence. "Now what?" I thought. "Well I will have to make the best of what I have while I try to transition into what I want and where my talents lie." I am still at the store; some for good reasons and others for bad like being lazy and not trying hard enough in my talents. But while God waited for me He said, "I will use you in this capacity, here at your store." And boy, did He ever. He transformed the store into a haven of a healthy financial business *and* the business of *His* love. Since I was "stuck" at the store, I decided to make loving people God's way a priority. It was then that our catch phrase, "we talk about politics and religion…", came into being. I wanted to do robust business but still talk about the things that society warns *not* to talk about.

I didn't see society moving in a positive direction, so I thought that if I didn't say anything then I was part of the problem. Not wanting to be guilty of complacency or a Nero imitator and fiddle as "Rome" burned down… I spoke, but listened as well. This is another learned trait that changed my life. Most of what I know is from listening. You can't really learn if you're the only one talking. When people were comfortable that I was genuinely hearing them, they started to open up in a more authentic way. By truly listening, I have seen the transformations I listed at the beginning of this chapter. As "souls started to gush," pain and sorrow was among the main themes. And I learned that no one is exempt.

I've listened to thousands of "gushing souls" across the spectrum- from encouraging or bizarre, to the dreadful. Throughout this book, I share several of the stories. I could share many hundreds more if I could remember all of them, but below are a few in a random, truncated version. As stated previously, I do not engage people on a spiritual level unless it comes up naturally, but when it does you get some pretty interesting comments such as these. For fun, I use a pseudo Clint Eastwood title and call this, "The Bad, The Odd, and The Good":

The Bad:

The guy who wanted to "blow my f**king head off";

Although this is not a "gushing souls" example where a customer opens up about their life, it is an example of dealing with people in a forthright and aggressive way when needed. An older 6'4" guy was on a nationwide crime spree that started in San Francisco. He traveled across the country with a teenage boy, taking advantage of anybody and everybody. His crime spree took him through Texas, Florida, and up the east coast to Maine where he tied and beat up an elderly couple in their home and stole their money and possessions. On his travel dossier one fine day, he purveyed our fine establishment. Rather than purchase anything, he decided to continue in his criminal ways and took out a HUGE gun and demanded I do what he says or he would blow my f**king head off. Simultaneously I drew my gun. Apparently, no one had ever stood up to him because when he saw my gun he about crapped himself and took off running. The police caught up to him a few minutes later and extradited him to Maine so the elderly couple could have their justice.

Another burly stranger that easily stood 6'4" and tipped the scales at over 300 lbs. came in to sell gold. He seemed depressed so I asked him if he was okay. He scowled, "What do you mean?" I said he looked upset and asked if I could do anything. He seemed annoyed and asked me if I was a Christian. I thought that was an odd question and was a bit wary to answer, but I never-the-less said, "Yep" ... I figured God is bigger than him so I should be alright. He said, "Okay, I will tell you my story." It was brutal. His young, teenage son got cancer and tragically died. They were driving home from the hospital and decided they didn't want to live in their home anymore- too many memories. They were devastated, depressed and blamed themselves. They bought an RV to run from themselves eventually ending up in our store telling us his story. The man sobbed deeply and told me they had been on the run for 3 months and had never shared their story with anyone. I was the first merely by reaching out and asking if I could help. I felt bad for having him relive the horror and apologized but he waved me off and said it was necessary and cathartic. I love kids and the story was exhausting to listen to, let alone having lived through it. I went home at 5:30 and slept the rest of the evening.

A young adult who I knew well and had several earthy conversations with came into the store to sell some silver... telling me he was selling to pay for his girlfriend's abortion. He knew my faith and position on this subject so I immediately addressed it. I said something like, "You know my position on abortion, so it seems you came in partly for me to tell you not to do that," and asked him if I was right. He agreed. Early in my life I was pro-choice, but after logically thinking it all the way through it became clear I was wrong. It is a growing baby- period. His family even did not yet know of his plight. I told him my strong objections and asked him to include his family in his decision. In the end he told his family and they did not abort the baby.

A fellow coin dealer came into our store often to buy coins. We had talked about Jesus on many occasions with him professing his love of the Lord. I saw him steal a coin and put it in his pocket, but he did not know I saw him. I said, "What's in your pocket?" He flushed, obfuscated, and lied. At the time we did not have video, so it would be my word against his if it went to court. So I asked him to leave. The next time he came in with a dozen roses, and acted as if nothing had happened. He said to give them to my lovely mother, to which I flatly responded, "Uh huh," and told him we had nothing for him and asked to leave again.

Even though people claim God's name or put a little fishy on their car doesn't mean that is really who they are. Unfortunately this is one of those "Christians" that non-believers observe and then determine *God* is no good. In actuality this man was just a thief, liar, covetous, hypocrite and God sees his heart, as it says in Psalm 44:21 and Luke 16:15.

Dave W. said he rejected the Catholic Church and a belief in God because he was not getting answers to fundamental questions. He saw the wrongs being committed and saw few rights. Initially he really was wanting to be involved with the church, but like me, he grew cold and then dead to the belief in God. I said to Dave, "You rejected the church for the right reasons, but rejected God for the wrong reasons." He saw the church people and the lives they hypocritically lived and equated them to God. It may be appropriate to leave a church because of pathetic "believers," but that is not a good reason to reject God. Remember, God is great but His people suck. Gandhi also has a saying attributed to him that is apropos, "I like their Christ. I don't like their Christian."

Along the same lines, an 80- year- old lady engaged in earthy conversation with me and eventually angrily blurted out in mid thought, "I didn't leave the church, the church left me." To this I said, "Amen." I knew exactly what she was talking about and have heard this from plenty of disillusioned churchized people. She maintained a belief in God, but became disillusioned with the stories preachers tell, and the lies, hate, and hypocrisy of the congregation. Ronald Reagan had a similar quote during his political career, "I didn't leave the Democrat Party, the Democratic Party left me."

The Odd:

One of the oddest situations happened in Atlanta. We were at a national coin show and a very funkafied lady approached our table and asked if we bought coins. She was really distinctive with a tight red and white, Where's Waldo-looking crop top, over an ample chest that was purposefully on display. She had bright red lips, dark, thick rimmed glasses, and half her head shaved with the other half being long blonde hair. Tattoos ran from her back, up her neck, into her shaved head and she had piercings galore. She slammed a couple albums onto our case and said meanly, "Here, look!" She was not a nice person. I tried to engage her in friendly banter but she was having none of it. She had wonderful coins that totaled $10,000. She was shocked. There were plenty of other dealers at this show and she said curtly, "I'm going to shop them around!" I said I understood. She was confused by my kindness and clandestinely sent a guy that was with her back to our table with coins she knew had no value. She told him to see if I was nice to him when he had nothing of value. At the time I didn't know he was with her. I try to be equally kind to everyone so he reported back to her that I was nice to him as well. She rapidly approached our table, slammed her albums again on the counter and said, "Buy the coins, but you weren't the highest price." I asked her why then would she sell them to me and she said, "Because the other guy was an asshole." (Don't get mad at me, Christians, I'm just relating a true story). Unfortunately I had forgotten my checkbook back in Pittsburgh and only had $8,000 from other dealers. I told her this and she said she wouldn't accept a check anyway because she didn't trust anyone. I tried to come to an agreement with her on picking out $8,000 worth of her coins and I would send her a check for the rest when I returned back to Pittsburgh. After the check cleared she could send me the rest of the coins. She said flatly, "No." I thought the deal was over until she slowly said, "I've never done this in my life." I said "What?" She said that she was going to let me take them all and send her a check for the remaining $2000. The "I've never done this…"

comment meant she had never trusted anyone. Tragic. What did this beautiful soul endure in her younger years? Must have been bad.

The story got a bit more weird. When I returned home and re-examined the collection, I saw that I missed an error on a coin that made it about $400 more than I told her. I thought if I sent her a check for an extra $400 she would not know why I did that, so I called her on the phone and explained why I would be sending her a check for $2400 rather than the promised $2000. Her response surprised me. She had a long pause, long enough that I wasn't sure if she was still on the phone. Then she *angrily* said, "PEOPLE DON'T DO THAT." Then it was my turn to pause because I thought a simple thank you was coming. Anger is not what I anticipated. I was confused… "People don't do what?" I said. "WHAT ARE YOU TRYING TO DO? What is your angle?" she asked. I didn't have an angle other than trying to do what was right. I wasn't put off by her anger or comments. I mostly thought about how horribly she must have been treated for most her life to be so caustic. I sent her $2400. She never thanked me. It's not in her vocabulary… yet. She may one day get there by a simple act of kindness. Perhaps I will see her in heaven and she will approach me and say, "Remember me?" and I'll say, "Nope!" (Because she probably would look different from when I first met her,) and she'll say "You were the first to help me establish trust in people again that eventually led me here." I can only hope.

Oddities in the store happen often. On several occasions people would be standing in the store and say, "I don't know why I am here." The first few times I approached them in a practical way by asking what they collect. Some would respond that they don't collect. So then it was my turn to ask why they were there. Eventually it seemed like God was sending them. Now I answer differently. An elderly, sophisticated black lady entered the store and just stood there looking lost. I asked if I could help and she blankly said, "I don't know why I am here." By this time I was used to this response, so I asked how she got there. She said God told her to come. She was interested in protecting her assets with gold and silver and that's what she eventually did.

On another occasion, a hardworking man came in and basically said that the Lord sent him to the store. He was extremely religious, charismatic, but practical and kind in his talking. He was very likable and we hit it off quickly. We met several times and on one of those meetings he casually said something close to, "There are two huge angels standing outside your store directing people into here." I said. "Uhhhh, ok." I couldn't possibly know if he was right. I haven't seen them, but there have been so many weird experiences that angels tossing people into the store could explain it.

An articulate, middle-aged man came in and wanted to sell a few things. As usual, we engaged in an earthy way. It was clear he was kind, smart, and easy to talk with. At some point in the conversation he asked if I was a Christian. I had said nothing of what I believed and didn't know why he asked this. He asked again and I said, "Yes, why?" Then he asked an unusual sort of reversed question, "Why didn't you try to preach at me when we were talking?" Notice his phrasing, "...preach AT me..." I told him flatly that it's not in my job description. I told him my job was to love first. Then I explained God's first two greatest commandments and his definition of love. Part of that definition is that love does not insist on its own way. When a Christian says, "I'm right and you are wrong, so listen up," they are placing themselves in a pretentious hierarchical position, thereby violating God's love because they are insisting on THEIR way.

To reiterate, I am not saying that all opinions are right! I'm simply saying we need to love by listening, regardless if we think what they are saying is wrong or ungodly. Love isn't the only thing, but it is the *first* thing in dealing with others. God's Word is full of commandments and harsh warnings and I'm perfectly willing to blast people with them IF they care to hear. I can't force their heart to hear.

So, I asked this guy what his occupation was and he said he plays the tuba for an orchestra. I asked him what he thought my response would be if he engaged me in tuba talk where he told me all about the tuba; where and who to take lessons from, how long to practice, how to improve, and where to get involved with other tuba-ers. He said I would likely *tune* out, (a little pun intended) and wonder why he was forcing his tuba on me. I said "Yep, that's why I don't preach AT people. I will only share what I believe while the other person shares what they believe." If people agree with what I am saying, they will check into it on a deeper level. This does not mean I think people such as street preachers are wrong. They are spreading the good news in their own special way. They are not insisting that people accept what they are saying, they are just shouting it from the "mountain tops." People can choose to ignore it if they want. I'm just talking about personal conversations.

Another of these personal conversations with a long-time customer came to an odd conclusion. He got a new job in California and stopped into the store to say his farewell. He did not believe in God but, since we had may exciting religious talks I asked him if he changed his mind. Surprisingly he said he had. Michael was an "Apple Genius" and was well spoken and very intelligent. He said, "I thought my way into agnosticism and I thought my way out." He accepted Jesus. This is what God asks us to do- seek him with your mind and do it with strength, (Luke 10:27).

The Good:

There have been so many good aspects of the store it would be impossible to list all of them. The highlights include the tears and pain turning to joy and laughter and seeing hope re-enter people's lives.

We have several customers that tell their family when they are headed to the store, "I'm off to church..." I love these comments. Kathy and Brian have been the most vocal about saying this. When Kathy told her husband that she was going to church at 2 pm on a Tuesday, he asked, "Where?" She said, "The coin store." I think he thinks she is nuts. But God says wherever two or more [faithful believers] are gathered, there he is with us (Matthew 18:20).

I'll share two final highlights: The first is when a lady was done doing business with us, she took several deep breaths while she smiled and looked around our simple store. She sighed and said, "It is so peaceful in here," and then left. But one of my candid favorites was something a lovely hippie lady who attended Woodstock stated. She had been in the store several times and we hit it off nearly right away. Every time she leaves the store she says, "I love you boys," and then says it again so we know she means it, "You know I love you." It's mutual. We love her too. But on one occasion after doing business she was headed out of the store and stopped before she got to the door. She slowly turned and looked forlorn. I was concerned and asked if she was okay. She said sadly, "I don't want to go out there," as she pointed outside the store. She said she feels at such peace in the store because she is loved that she doesn't want to exit into an angry world that doesn't care about her. She is so right. The world is angry. If only we would all see the truth in God's definition of love and practice it. It would be a world that we would want to live in.

5

Christians... meh

Sometimes "Christian," seems more like a dirty moniker on a name-patch of a grease monkey's coveralls than a real description of followers of Christ. Those who truly understand this title of 'Christian,' know that our jobs are to be more like God and progressively less and less like our former greasy selves. (No disrespect to my fellow greasers. I like to break and fix stuff like the rest of you.) The only way to be more like Him is to read His Word, pray, argue with each other in love, and talk about real life issues rather than the weather. God's promise is that as we draw closer to Him, He will draw closer to us: James 4:8, *"Draw near to God, and he will draw near to you. Cleanse your hands, you sinners, and purify your hearts, you double-minded."*

So, Christian intentions should be drawing closer to God. However, generally speaking, it's been my observation that Christians have a parochial view of God. We are like little children who just want to play and never grow up- like Peter Pan. Hebrews 5:12-13 *slams* this childish Christian, saying, *"For though by this time you ought to be teachers, you need someone to teach you again the basic principles of the oracles of God. You need milk, not solid food, for everyone who lives on milk is unskilled in the word of righteousness, since he is a child."*

It appears Christians are content with their mediocrity and ignorance of God's Word and how it relates to the world. Since we don't know His Word, we can't live by it or defend it appropriately. Instead, we naively make up stuff that is NOT biblical and try to hoodwink people into believing it: then when non-Christians hear it, they respond with justified confusion and indignation.

Worse yet it seems Christians have come to be influenced by, and have accepted, the ways of the secular world over God's Word. We know more about actors, movie scenes, and singers' lyrics than the words of Jesus. Christians, if you can sing along to worldly songs, but not quote as many lines from the Bible, your heart and head are in the wrong place! James 4:4 sternly warns; *"You adulterous people! Do you not know that friendship with the world is enmity with God? Therefore whoever wishes to be a friend of the world makes himself an enemy of God."* That verse is talking to Christians, not non-believers. So stop your worldly ways or you will be an *enemy* of God! When we lose God's perspective by not knowing His Word, we live a type of pseudo-Christianity by intermixing with worldly ways. When you live this pseudo-Christian way, you speak pseudo-Christianese. Then when you bloviate about being a Christian, you're non-believing friends think, "And that's why I'm not one." It would be like your neighbor seeing you return home from church, all churchy dressed up, screaming at your kids as you get out of the car. Then you glance over and see your neighbor- give him a cute neighborly wave and say he should come to church with you the next Sunday, then tell him to have a "blessed day"- as you turn your ire back to your wife and kids.

This pseudo-Christianese then manifests itself through hypocrisy and judgmentalism. "You're not supposed to judge me." I have heard this numerous times from non-Christians and Christians alike, yet it is *Christians* who almost universally get this 180 degrees backwards. They are quick to judge the non-Christian as "sinners," but when they are judged by other Christians, they often say "don't judge me." One of the main criticisms of Christians by non-Christians is they hate it when we judge them, and they are right in hating this! If a non-Christian says, "don't judge me", he would be correct! We are called to love the people in the world, not judge them. If someone DOES NOT claim to love or follow God, how dare WE judge and hold them to His standards? That's His job. God specifically says this in 1 Corinthians 5:12-13, *"What business is it of mine to judge those outside the church? Are you not to judge those inside? God will judge those outside. 'Expel the wicked person from among you.'"* Christians, when you judge the world, you are placing yourself in God's role, and are rightly condemned with indignation from secular society. When God tells us that it is His job to judge the unbelievers, we should be perfectly content with that. Who can judge better than God, the perfect creator of human thought, emotion and being?

So we are not to directly judge non-Christians and we *are* to judge each other, but how? When I asked Christians in an adult Bible class I teach whether it is right to judge, the majority of them said no. They are partially correct. We ARE supposed to judge those who claim the name of Christ as their Savior. When Jesus healed someone on the sabbath, the crowd was very angry about this and he said to them, *"Stop judging by mere appearances, but instead judge correctly,"* (John 7:24). If we weren't supposed to judge he wouldn't say, "Judge correctly." Also, Matthew 7:1-5 and Luke 6:37-41 say, *"Do not judge, or you too will be judged."* If we stop there, the answer seems to be that we are not supposed to judge, but, it goes on…

> *For in the same way you judge others, you will be judged, and with the measure you use, it will be measured to you. Why do you look at the speck of sawdust in your brother's eye and pay no attention to the plank in your own eye? How can you say to your brother, "Let me take the speck out of your eye," when all the time there is a plank in your own eye? You hypocrite, first take the plank out of your own eye, and then you will see clearly to remove the speck from your brother's eye.*

So, in the end, this is actually telling us TO judge, but to be very careful of whom and how we judge! We must FIRST look at our own hearts and make sure we are not engaging in the sin on which we are judging our own brothers and sisters. If you are a liar, don't judge someone for lying, but if you have excellent control over your tongue and do not lie, then by all means- have at it and call out the brothers'/sisters' lies.

The apostle Paul gives us an example of judging those inside the church, as he harshly did to a Christian guy who was having sex with his "father's wife." In 1 Corinthians 5:1, Paul excoriated the church for tolerating this and said that this type of behavior wouldn't even happen in the pagan world. *"...You are to deliver this man over to Satan for the destruction of the flesh,"* Paul continued to say. This does not mean that the person is forever condemned; they are, however, to be withdrawn from the church until they repent, (1 Corinthians 5:2). Luke 17:3 says, *"Pay attention to yourselves! If your brother sins, rebuke him, and if he repents, forgive him..."* There are many other verses that talk about rebuking a believer in order to bring them to repentance. The main one is Matthew 18:15-17 where it gives the whole process of rebuking, repenting and forgiving. Christians, if you don't know this passage you should read it.

So, we must be careful in how we judge other Christians. Occasionally I have heard Christians rebuke other Christians in a very caustic, holier-than-thou, vitriolic way, which is clearly wrong. The Bible says to rebuke in love. They are to do this in order to restore the believer, leading them to repentance, not to disown or embarrass them. We are in this game together and are to hold each other accountable so the Word of God will not be maligned.

There is a caveat to non-Christians whining about Christians judging them, however. Christians are required *not* to keep their faith to themselves. Matthew 10:27 tells them to shout about the good news from the housetops. If a non-believer feels judged from them openly sharing God's Word publicly, then the non-believer's blame is misplaced. If then the non-believer says, "You're not supposed to judge me," the Christian should say, "I'm not. I'm simply quoting God's Word by which you are feeling convicted and therefore judged. So it is not me who is judging you, but God's truth." Additionally, having said that Christians aren't to judge the world doesn't mean that we don't believe in and espouse God's Word. If someone is offended at God's Word- GOOD! We don't have to accept or *tolerate* humanists' whims and abhorrent behaviors. So how do we do that without judging? The difference is in the sin versus the person sinning. The sin has already been condemned by God, but the sinner hasn't... at least until he or she draws their final breath.

In addition to wrongful judgmentalism, Christian ignorance of God's Word is a vexing problem. It is fertile ground for Satan who DOES know God's Word and uses it to confuse and manipulate believers into further misrepresenting God. Satan intermingles truth with lies to encourage believers to sin. Eve is an example of this when she was instructed by God not to touch the tree of good and evil knowledge. In Genesis 3:4-5 Satan told Eve a lie. Verse 4 shows the lie by saying she would not die if she ate the fruit; verse 5 states the partial truth- that her eyes would be opened to good and evil after she ate. Christians often don't know God's Word because they don't bother to read it, which in turn gives Satan ground to trick unknowledgeable Christians into bastardizing, misquoting and adding to it.

But you can't blame the Christian, can you? After all, there is social media to keep up with, hair and makeup that need attention, sport stats to memorize, gossip to catch up on, alcohol to guzzle, poor people to ignore or tell to have a blessed day, shopping sprees, divorce care to attend at church then shuttle your pawn children to your ex's, selfies to take...you know important stuff that takes an exhausting amount of time. Christians who don't have time for God's Word have their priorities backasswards. As a result of not knowing and living by God's Word, church attendance overall is plummeting and atheism and hatred of Christians is on the rise. The evidence of this?: divorce, drug addiction, out of wedlock births, and lawsuits, are similar in numbers between Christians and non-Christians. Christians, we suck because we have failed to know God through knowing His Word and place Him *always* before our own desires.

There are several areas where Christians' lack of knowledge of God's Word has profoundly affected and hurt the church. One among many blatantly obvious problems in the church is divorce. God says He *hates* divorce, yet the church regrettably ignores God's Word and participates in this desecration! Oddly we have programs like "divorce care" in the church- I see it advertised in most major church bulletins and placards. "*Divorce* care" though?! Wouldn't "*pre*-divorce care" be a Godlier alternative?! Yet I have never seen this advertised in a church bulletin. This acceptance of divorce by the church then lends to an additional sin which is lawsuits between believers. The Bible couldn't be clearer that we are NOT to sue other believers. A divorce *is* a lawsuit; there is a plaintiff and a defendant in the divorce papers.

1 Corinthians 6:1-9 says:

If any of you has a dispute with another, do you dare to take it before the ungodly for judgment instead of before the Lord's people? Or do you not know that the Lord's people will judge the world? And if you are to judge the world, are you not competent to judge trivial cases? 3 Do you not know that we will judge angels? How much more the things of this life! Therefore, if you have disputes about such matters, do you ask for a ruling from those whose way of life is scorned in the church? I say this to shame you. Is it possible that there is nobody among you wise enough to judge a dispute between believers? But instead, one brother takes another to court—and this in front of unbelievers! The very fact that you have lawsuits among you means you have been completely defeated already. Why not rather be wronged? Why not rather be cheated? Instead, you yourselves cheat and do wrong, and you do this to your brothers and sisters. Or do you not know that wrongdoers will not inherit the kingdom of God?

Lawsuits are public events carried out in front of a secular judge, attorneys, et al. This *should be* demoralizing to us because it is ultimately mocking God. We demonstrate hatred rather than love towards each other and put it on full public display in the courts and the secular world. God is really the one on trial because we are His representatives. The non-believing world looks at us tearing each other and our families apart and would rightly conclude, "... if these people are Christians, then no thanks…" It clearly demonstrates to the world a good reason NOT to believe. But since divorce is such a big problem *within* the church it also shows how horrific a job the church is doing convincing believers of the basic tenets of God's Word. If believers are not supposed to sue each other, how are serious problems supposed to be resolved? God's Word has the answer for this which the Christian church appears to ignore. For the sake of boring some readers I put a synopsis of a Bible study I taught in the back of the book (addendum 1).

Continuing to illustrate Christians' self-imposed ignorance is the non-biblical nonsense that is espoused in Christian books. Not fitting the conventional Christian mold, I have been given many books from people trying to help me and bring me back into the fold… you know, saving my wayward soul. That's when I came to the realization that there is a lot of horse hooey disguised as godly advice. I mean there is some really awful, unbiblical stuff written by Christians and published by Christian book companies and organizations. Many of these books are nearly completely the author's *opinion* and have few to no references of God's Word. Even if there are references, often they are out of context or pieced together to fit the author's narrative. It's ironic that this book, *God is Great but His People Suck*, would most likely not be published by a Christian organization because of the title. But throughout this entire book I reference God's Word because this is a book about Him and why I believe He is the Truth, the Light and the Way… but His people suck. Plus, as I said, "Who cares what I think." There are some inspiring books written that I'm sure please God, but if a Christian book does not point the reader to God using God's Word, then it should be pointed to the trash.

As an example of some nonsense that can be in these so called "Christian" books, I read one written by a woman to men, talking about how to please a woman. It was published by a very respectable Christian organization. It was so awful that I wondered if anyone read it before publishing. It actually endorses *lying* to your wife and treating her like a fairytale princess to please her, so the husband can have better sex. She tells husbands to write the word "perfect" on sticky notes and put it on the bathroom scale. So, if your wife is a lazy 300- pound glutton, tell her she is perfect! In 1 Corinthians 6:19, it talks about the body being a temple for the Holy Spirit. Perhaps she misunderstood the meaning and thought she needed to be the *size* of a temple. The Bible talks about putting healthy things in your body and to keep it fit. For those who may say I'm "fat shaming," you're misplacing the blame. God is fat "shaming." And for those who respond to this in shock and horror, lighten up. If you can't laugh at yourself then don't laugh… at anything. No matter what the "joke" is, someone could take offense. Plus I don't think being fat is any worse a sin than gossip or other "lesser" sins. It is just more overtly noticeable and unbecoming of a Christian.

Another book's advice from a pastor was how to *leave* your husband because he's not emotionally supportive. It instructs the woman to berate her husband and, "don't let him speak a word," if the husband dares to try and ask questions while she is lecturing him. I could write an entire book on the plethora of really crappy "advice" is in Christian books, and also for that matter, spoken from Christian pulpits. This is why we need to read and know God's Word for ourselves, so we can discern if we are hearing questionable teaching and preaching.

Beyond the unhealthy advice of Christian authors are the detrimental words coming from pulpits. Church denominations and its leaders go beyond God's Word, making up their own traditions and fabrications, which the sheeple blindly follow. There are numerous reasons why Christians fabricate their own belief system. I surmise a few of the main ones would be ignorance of God's Word (as discussed above), to satisfy their sinful life, or to gain financial advantage and control over a larger group of people. It is dangerous to add or take away from God's Word as ominously warned about in Revelations 22:18. "Here, roll these baubles between your fingers and say these incantations and you and God will be buddies again." Things like this aren't in the Bible or even suggested but can be used to make the "flock" feel better without people actually having to take personal responsibility for their lives. But Philippians 4:6 says, *"Do not be anxious about anything, but in everything by prayer and supplication with thanksgiving let your requests be made known to God."* It's clear that we should not take our concerns and sins to man for forgivingness but directly to God. Now if we want to take our concerns, difficulties or sins to people in order to get help, that's terrific! But a human can't absolve you of your sins, only God can.

Another example of a tradition that I believe is often misused or overused is the Lord's Prayer and prayer in general. I think that, too often, Christians get lulled into a false sense of satisfaction with God because we offer up simple prayers such as the "Lord's Prayer" every Sunday or we pray before a meal, as a couple minor examples. Thanking

God for your food is a positive thing, but why not thank Him for each breath you take because without that, you wouldn't be eating!

When you say the same thing over and over, it naturally becomes dull and meaningless. If you listened to your favorite song every day for weeks, months and years, you would wonder why you even liked the song to begin with! I actually think the "Lord's Prayer" should be called the "Lord's blueprint." Matthew 6:5-7 says:

> *When you pray you must not be like the hypocrites. For they love to stand and pray in the synagogues, and the street corners, that they can be seen by others. Truly, I say to you, they have received their reward. But when you pray, go into your room and shut the door and pray to your Father who is in secret. And your Father who sees in secret will reward you. And when you pray, do not heap up empty phrases as the Gentiles do, for they think they will be heard for their many words. Do not be like them, for your Father knows what you need before you ask him. Pray then like this: "Our Father in heaven…"*

As a twist of irony, when a congregation stands and recites the "Lord's Prayer," they may be "heaping up empty phrases" because it has become such a monotonous routine that it is not actually being prayed, but meaninglessly recited. Jesus was establishing a *blueprint* of things to be thankful for. In Matthew 6:9, Jesus says, "pray then *like* this," not, "pray these exact words." Praying "the Lord's Prayer", it's not wrong unless you're doing it because, "everyone else is." Paul says to pray unceasingly, in 1 Thessalonians 5:16-17. I think this keeps our prayers exciting and fresh and more appreciative of what God has provided. So yes, thank Him for your food…and breath, health, abilities, nature, animals, friends, sex, water, mitochondrial activity, chemical elements...you know...basically everything...all the time. When you keep learning about the myriad intricacies of what He created, you will never run out of things to thank Him for! And for those of you who have many problems or ailments, I understand it's considerably more difficult to thank God, but that doesn't mean there's *nothing* to thank Him for. Start by thanking Him for simple things like water or breath. The more things you thank Him for, you will realize what you have and what you have taken for granted.

So, Christians, it's time to stop looking at fishy crackers with a cross on it, or "blood" weeping statues as miraculous signs from God, and appreciate the true signs from God which are His nature, your body, the heavens, etc. Stop making your own stuff up and then cursing God when it doesn't go your way. Life rarely goes as we planned and it goes even worse when we unwittingly live by our own ways rather than God's ways. Ironically, Christians who live by their own rules and blame God when they fail are a lot like non-Christians who say they DON'T believe in God... yet curse Him. Cursing God is easy. Rather than providing the scapegoat, now He has become the scapegoat. When I went to the funeral of a lady's son (whom I loved), she told me she blames my God for his death. Yet for decades she stated boldly that there is no God. It would have been inappropriate for me to respond at that time, but how in the world can you blame something you don't believe in?! To me this says she really does believe He exists, she just doesn't want to play by His rules.

Most people don't want to play by God's rules. But what is worse; someone who states they don't believe in God and does their own thing, or someone who says they do believe in God but plays by the world's rules? The answer is clear. The non-believer may be wrong, but at least they aren't the hypocrite. Many thoughts and opinions that Christians have are based on their pious, conservative, cultural upbringing and not biblically based. For example, Las Vegas is a place where every sin imaginable to humanity is found, every day; it isn't called Sin City for nothing! But, when my daughter found inexpensive plane tickets to Las Vegas and called me asking if I wanted to write a large part of this book there, I jumped at the opportunity. I had been to Las Vegas one other time and loved the activity, lights, glitz, glamour, shows, and people. I was excited to go back! Las Vegas is also a land of degradation, seediness, crime, pornography strewn streets, corruption, theft, opulence, gambling, drugs, despair, rape, murder, drunkenness, suicide, hopelessness, hate… you know… the place that Jesus would be found if he was on the earth today, (Mark 2:16-17). I was warned to avoid this place by other Christians. Honestly, that's as dumb as warning me not to live on earth since the exact same seedy things are throughout the world. Jesus said three times in John 17:14-18 that Christians are not of this world, but we have to live in it, just like he did. Can you get trapped by Vegas' enticing ways? For sure! However, I have had numerous arguments with Christians about the main "sins" they often point to about the problems of Vegas- gambling, alcohol, lust, and opulence. These things are NOT biblically prohibited (except lust), but many Christians project their religiosity onto them, making God seem stringent and prudish. As I said, God is no prude, His people are. God establishes guidelines to efficiently work within the world He created for our benefit, not to piss us off.

Let's look at four Vegas "sins" that Christians get themselves worked up over and see what God actually has to say about them.

First: Gambling. I don't personally gamble because it's just not fun for me. I'm also proficient enough at math to know that gambling is not a **smart** money-making plan. However, gambling is not biblically wrong… the love of money is. Ecclesiastes 5:10 simply states that a person who loves money will never be satisfied and it eventually leads to vanity. Gambling can LEAD to wrong-doing if you spend more than you've budgeted for fun. But saying gambling is wrong because people often spend more than they can afford would be the same illogic if someone said that food was wrong because some people eat too much and get fat.

I can now hear the chorus of Christian dissenters to this opinion. They would be saying, people have to eat but they don't have to gamble and waste money. To them I say put your money where your mouth is. If you own ANYTHING; a house, car, tv, computer, cell phones, books, tables, lamps, dressers or clothes, you should sell it ALL as per the instructions of Jesus in Matthew 19:21 where he says, *"If you would be perfect, go, sell what you possess and give to the poor, and you will have treasure in heaven; and come and follow me."* In verse 23 He says it is with significant difficulty a rich man may enter heaven, but this is not because you *have* stuff, it's because you covet it (Luke 12:15). Moreover Christians, if you still want to continue with your piety and fault finding, then buy out of date generic food, don't go on vacation, never eat out, cancel your cell phone plan, live in a tent (or better yet a cave), and certainly no Starbucks!

Also, alcohol is not wrong. In fact, on rare occasions God endorses getting drunk! I know this will send pious Christians into an apoplectic lather, but to quell their frothing I will quote Proverbs 31:6: *"Give strong drink to the one who is perishing and wine to those in bitter distress; let them drink and forget their poverty and remember their misery no more."* God gives plenty of warnings about getting drunk and states clearly that in most situations it is wrong. 1 Corinthians 6:9-10 says drunkards will not inherit the kingdom of heaven. Even though it doesn't say it, I think it is safe to say that drug addicts would be in the same category. But it definitely is not wrong to drink alcohol. If it were wrong then I'm pretty sure Jesus' first miracle would not have been changing water into wine while being encouraged to do so by his mother, Mary! (John 2:1-11). In fact, it is not hard to surmise that many of the wedding guests would have already been tipsy because the master of the banquet says in verse 10, *"Why did you save the best wine for last?"* (the wine that Jesus made.) The best wine was usually served first and after the guests were tipsy, the cheap wine would be served since at that point they wouldn't care what it tasted like. Also we know that Jesus drank wine when he said that John the Baptist did not drink wine, but he did himself and was (erroneously) called a drunkard. There are several other verses that encourage drinking alcohol: Ecclesiastes 9:7 instructs, *"Go, eat your bread with joy, and drink your wine with a merry heart, for God has already approved what you do."* Psalm 104:14-15 says that God gives wine to *"gladden the heart of man..."* In fact the Bible goes even further and tells people not to only drink water, but drink wine as well *"for the ails of your stomach,"* (1 Timothy 5:3).

Again, I am not encouraging getting drunk; God knows that alcohol can be dangerous and addicting, which is why He gives us the boundary about not getting drunk. Yet, God gives allowances to drink responsibly and on very rare occasions to get blitzed when we are in deep suffering, because He cares for us. Again this shows that our awesome God is not the prude… His people are.

Lust is wrong, but what is it? What's the level that tips it to sin? Appreciating God's creation of the body is not wrong, but what do you do with the thoughts? In 2 Samuel 11:2-27 King David saw Bathsheba bathing naked on her roof, which was not wrong. He noticed that she was an attractive woman which is a natural response that God created in us. If he had stopped there and said, "Wow, is she a fine little lamb," (you know, that's what they used to say back in the day), David would have been on the safe side of God's law, but NOPE, David was KING and at that moment placed himself higher than God's law. David knew better… but Bathsheba was fiiiiiiiiine, so he lusted, placing himself on the other side of God's law. So what was the tipping point into lust? David's vision of beauty crossed into ungodly lust when his thoughts became an active mental pursuit. As a result of his lust, he sent his guards for her, had sex, got her pregnant, lied to her husband, got him drunk so he would have sex with his wife in an effort to cover up the pregnancy, and ultimately had her husband put to death. James 1:14-15 says, *"But each person is tempted when he is lured by his own desire. Then desire gives birth to sin, and sin when it is fully grown brings forth death."*

Solomon, David's son, talked a considerable amount about his lover's body, especially her breasts on several occasions. *"Your two breasts are like…"* If you want to be entertained, read *The Song of Solomon*, starting in chapter four. His description of his lover would not be the words we use today, such as; *"Your lips are like a scarlet thread, and your mouth is lovely. Your cheeks are like halves of a pomegranate"* …but you get the idea. We might make fun of Solomon's words today but it is a poetic, oddly worded, yet beautiful love letter, unlike today's crassness where one might say, "Nice tits, are they real?" God created our physical bodies and said that they were good. He created us to be emotional, spiritual, physical and sexual beings, so recognizing, appreciating, and desiring God's creation, *within* His boundaries, is NOT wrong.

Finally, opulence is not wrong. God gives grand blessings of wealth to His people. Abraham had enormous wealth and so did Solomon and many other biblical patriarchs. God cares about what you *do* with that wealth, NOT that you have it. King Solomon's wealth was so vast that 2 Chronicles 1:15 says silver and gold were as common as stones in the city. **Just like Solomon's kingdom,** the United States is the most prosperous country in the world and gives more to the world than any other nation. To be in a position to give so generously the US needed to create a system of charity. The US recognized tyranny, tried through dialogue to end it, created a new government based on basic rights for humanity, fought a painful war to free its people from it, busted their asses through intensely difficult labor to enhance freedom, created phenomenal wealth as a result, and THEN was in a position to give

81

generously to the rest of the world… which we have. (For you naysayers, yes, we have done some wrong, but that does not negate the above facts).

Opulence can, however, lead to destruction. Eventually Solomon's wealth went outside of God's parameters by assuming he was better than others, along with *many* other foibles. (in a similar way to today's Christians). As a result, Solomon suffered enormously, and eventually (wrongly) concluded, like most people today, that all of life is vain (Ecclesiastes 1:2). Opulence is wrong when you can't afford it. This doesn't mean just taking care of yourself. God asks for you to give to His purposes *first,* such as financially supporting the church, but then includes taking care of widows, orphans, and the poor. If you have vast wealth and are spending it all on yourself you are clearly outside of God's Word. He says, *"Everyone to whom much was given, of him much will be required…"* in Luke 12:48 and earlier in the same chapter, He says, *"Sell your possessions, and give to the needy. Provide yourselves with moneybags that do not grow old, with a treasure in the heavens that does not fail, where no thief approaches and no moth destroys,"* (verse 33).

The United States is vastly wealthy, but being the most prosperous nation on earth with tens of trillions dollar in debt without a plan or idea to pay it back is not only oxymoronic, but *immoral.* We are placing a massive debt on our kids. If Christians are living a lifestyle beyond their means like our country is, then they are outside of God's Word. If they are in debt, how can they help others? It is actually selfish. They are hurting themselves, their family, and their community. How can they help others if they can't help themselves? Also, this is not a "prosperity gospel" endorsement where some pastors have erroneously said that all true Christians should be wealthy. To them I would ask, why then did Jesus say the poor woman who dropped a "penny" (mite) into the offering plate gave more than all the wealthy people?

Once again, Christians, we must accept God's parameters for living and stop making up our own. When we make up our own rules about what is right and wrong, we do not accurately represent our God who is perfectly good and cares deeply about the world. He sets up boundaries for our protection because He loves us, not because He is a strict, oppressive Ruler. We need to, as Jesus said in John 17, be in the world but not of it. Las Vegas' beguiling ways do not tempt me, so it was the perfect place for me to start this controversial book. I can enjoy being there, but not feel compelled to participate in its worst aspects. I am in love with Vegas and its people. I thank God for the myriad of talented people that took a desert and turned it into an oasis. Whether people recognize God or not, they recognized their God-given talents and employed them, becoming inventors, architects, city planners, businesses, actors, singers, dancers, artists of all types, restaurateurs, waiters, nurses, and maids, to create such an amazing place. In other words, it's all of God's gifts on parade. In a place like Vegas, I only see opportunity… no, not to "win big," but to love people as God asked me to. Matthew 5:43-47 says,

> You have heard that it was said, "You shall love your neighbor and hate your enemy." But I say to you, Love your enemies and pray for those who persecute you, so that you may be sons of Your Father who is in heaven. For he makes his sun rise on the evil and on the good, and sends rain on the just and on the unjust. For if you love those who love you, what reward do you have? Do not even the tax collectors do the same? And if you greet only your brothers, what more are you doing than others? Do not even the Gentiles do the same? You therefore must be perfect, as your heavenly Father is perfect.

You can love God in Vegas or wherever you are. We can choose to play His "game" of life or we can gamble (eh heh) and play by our own rules. Ultimately though, when it comes right down to it, we really don't trust God or care what He has to say. As an example, if you burn your hand on a hot stove, you know the severe pain. The likelihood of you doing that again is slim because it hurt so much you will obviously be very cautious the next time you encounter a hot stove. The analogy is like sin. We "burn" God when we sin. But what is the chance we will keep burning Him by sinning? Highly likely! Why? If we are being honest, it's because we care more about ourselves than God. So, we are placing *ourselves* above God. We hurt ourselves and say, "Ow! I'm not doing that again." We hurt God and we say, "whatever."

God doesn't set up rules to have us fail. They're set up so that we can live a fulfilling life. He knows that once we step outside of His suggestions, we are hurting ourselves, our friends, our family, our society and worst of all, Him. I purposefully used the word "suggestions," because anyone is free to break them. *Initially* God only had one "suggestion" when He first created the world: don't eat of ONE tree. He even told what the consequences would be if we did, *"...you will surely die,"* (Genesis 2:17). We were *allowed* to choose His way *OR* our own way. We can choose to accept His love or reject Him. But when Christians claim to love Him and DON'T choose His ways, we hold His ways up to contempt, basically saying, "Yeah I hear ya, but I don't really care." Again, I believe this *rightly* gives the world grounds for mockery of Christians. Non-Christians are quick to notice these inconsistencies of word and deed. We have been, and are, poor representatives of God. We need to place God first and seek His ways before anything else.

Christians, because we don't trust God and take the things that He says seriously, we deny His power, or at least that He is willing to use it. As an example, I was in a meaningful Bible study with a bunch of dedicated, manly dudes. One of the fellas has MS which causes him a lot of debilitating pain. He was feeling it at one of the studies and one of the guys suggested we should pray for his pain. I said, "Count me out. I'm not praying for his pain to go away." I got a couple quizzical looks 'cause I sounded like a jerk, (or as they say in Pittsburgh, a "jag-off"). I said that if God was powerful enough to remove his pain, He is powerful enough to remove the infirmity completely. Why limit God? Jesus said that if we had the faith of a mustard seed we could move mountains, (Matthew 17:20.) This was an answer to his disciples' question when they couldn't heal someone. And Jesus followed it up by saying, *"Nothing would be impossible for you."* James 4:3 takes it further and says, *"You ask and do not receive because you ask wrongly…"*

Miraculous answers to prayer are rare, but we need to keep asking God for them. However, there are many churches today who deny God's power because they don't see miracles happen and thus conclude that it was for another time in history. Nowhere in the Bible does it say this. Perhaps they feel weak because they are not able to perform miracles, so they come up with an excuse. I have personally not healed anyone… yet. It's possible that I won't be able to because it is a spiritual gift. But I will strive toward a mustard seed faith so that one day I might be able to heal the sick or blind. If you deny God's power, He surely will deny it to you. Before Jesus died, he said in John 14:12 that we would do greater works than Him. Again, if we don't believe that, we won't.

Another area where we don't believe in God's power or Word is when He asks us to be perfect. (I don't think God is holding His breath on this one however). When this is pointed out to Christians, their first reaction is to say, "That's impossible." If that were true, then why does God ask that of us? Are you saying God's Word is false? Matthew 5:48 says, *"You therefore must be perfect, as your Heavenly Father is perfect."*

If Christians deny God's Word and say we cannot be perfect by retraining ourselves from sin, then ask- Are you sinning right now? How about the next minute, or the minute after that, or the one after that? At what minute are you going to sin? And then at that minute I will ask you, "Why?" If you say you can't stop sinning, I'd mostly agree with you. You surely can't if you've convinced yourself you can't. In fact, you wouldn't try. Would you? But, I say, give it a chance. Minute by minute, hour by hour, day by day. Reach for the perfection that God asks of us, because He has already empowered you to do so! Romans 8:26 says, *"In the same way, the Spirit helps us in our weakness…"* God has called us to perfection, relying on His power each and every day. We need to stop making up excuses, stop sinning, and trust God and His Word. 1 Peter 4:15-16 says, *"But as He who called you is holy, you also be holy in ALL your conduct, because it is written, 'Be holy, for I am holy.'"*

In Philippians 3:12-14, Paul says, *"I don't mean to say that I have already achieved these things or that I have already reached perfection. But I press on to possess that perfection for which Christ Jesus first possessed me. No, dear brothers and sisters, I have not achieved it, but I focus on this one thing: Forgetting the past and looking forward to what lies ahead, I press on to reach the end of the race and receive the heavenly prize for which God, through Christ Jesus, is calling us."*

Here are other verses to look up if you want to learn more about perfection: Colossians 1:28, 4:12, Hebrews 12:23, James 2:22, 1 John 4:16-17, Romans 6:1-22 (focus on verses 6, 7, 12, 13, 14, 18, 22), Romans 8:2-17, James 1:4, and 2 Peter 1:9-10.

Although God asks us to trust Him and strive for perfection, it is not easy to do! Following God's requirements in a fallen world is difficult! Life is harsh. God actually promised that life would be arduous after we screwed Him by our original sin in the Garden of Eden and continue to live in a broken world because of our sin. As a result of not doing things His way, our hearts and minds get twisted and confused. Numerous verses tell us this:

- *"Everyone utters lies to his neighbor; with flattering lips and a double heart they speak,"* (Psalm 12:2).

- *"The heart is deceitful above all things, and desperately sick; who can understand it?"* (Jeremiah 17:9-10).

- *"For we all stumble in many ways…"* (James 3:2).

- *"…envy makes bones rot,"* (Proverbs 14:30).

- *"And the tongue is a fire, a world of unrighteousness. The tongue is set among our members, staining the whole body, setting on fire the entire course of life, and set on fire by hell. For every kind of beast and bird, of reptile and sea creature, can be tamed and has been tamed by mankind, but no human being can tame the tongue. It is a restless evil, full of deadly poison. With it we bless our Lord and Father, and with it we curse people who are made in the likeness of God. From the same mouth come blessing and cursing,"* (James 3:6-10).

- *"Jesus said, 'For from within, out of the heart of man, come evil thoughts, sexual immorality, theft, murder, adultery, coveting, wickedness, deceit, sensuality, envy, slander, pride, foolishness. All these evils come from within, and they defile a person,'"* (Mark 7:21).

- *"Jesus said to them, 'You are those who justify yourselves before men, but God knows your hearts. For what is exalted among men is an abomination in the sight of God,'"* (Luke 16:15).

- *"Every way of man is right in his own eyes, but the Lord weighs the heart,"* (Proverbs 21:2).

Satan is that "twister" of hearts and minds. Christians, you are not safe just because you believe. Satan will mess with your head if you don't guard against him. But he can't do anything to you if *you* don't let him! James 4:7 says, *"Resist the devil, and he will flee from you."* So how do Christians guard against being twisted and confused? There are many verses that cover this, but here is a basic outline about how to be discerning and stand against Satan:

Preliminary steps:

- One must be a born-again believer to have any connection to the will of God, (John 3:16, Romans 10:9).

- Receive the free gift of the Holy Spirit, (Acts 2:38).

- The Holy Spirit will act as an intercessor between you and God so that you can discern between God's right and wrong, (Romans 8:26-27).

Then there is a process of testing ourselves and committing to learning and practicing these things:

- **LOVE**, is by far the most important commitment:
- Love God with all your heart, mind and soul, (Mark 12:30).
- The definition of love, (1 Corinthians 13:4-8).
- *"Whoever does not love does not know God,"* (1 John 4:8).

- Obtain wisdom:

- *"The fear of the Lord is the beginning of wisdom, and the knowledge of the holy is understanding,"* (Proverbs 9:10).
- *"If any of you lacks wisdom, you should ask God, who gives generously to all without finding fault, and it will be given to you. But when you ask, you must believe and not doubt, because the one who doubts is like a wave of the sea, blown and tossed by the wind,"* (James 1:5-6).

- Commit every thought captive to Christ, (1 Corinthians 10:5).

- Use the Word of God as reproof, (2 Timothy 3:16).

- Test yourself using the Word of God, (Romans 12:2).

- Know the Word of God, (1 Peter 3:15).
- *"Man shall not live on bread alone, but from every word that comes from the mouth of God,"* (Matthew 4:4).

- Pray and fast, (Matthew 6:16-18).
- Jesus prayed and fasted for forty days to withstand Satan, (Matthew 4:2).

- Listen to wise counsel- not necessarily the people with the degrees from universities or theological seminaries, but Godly, *wise* people, (Proverbs 19:20).

- Compare what people say to the Word of God so you are not led astray, (2 Peter 2:1-3).

- Put on the armor of God, (Ephesians 6:10-18).

Additionally, Christians, be careful that you do not profess God without truly knowing and pursuing Him. Many who claim to believe in God are going to be very surprised in the end, thinking they have a ticket to heaven, and finding out in the worst way that they were gravely mistaken. Matthew 7:21-23 gives the ominous warning:

> *Not everyone who says to me, "Lord, Lord," will enter the kingdom of heaven, but the one who does the will of my Father who is in heaven. On that day, many will say to me, 'Lord, Lord, did we not prophesy in your name, and cast out demons in your name, and do many mighty works in your name?' And then will I declare to them, "I never knew you; depart from me, you workers of lawlessness."*

We all go through difficulties, usually every day. God says He puts us through difficult times because He loves us. On the face of it this sounds contradictory, but if you think it through, it is logical. What coach would allow their athlete in training to not practice because it's too hard? They push them to be the best. No athlete thanks their coach for letting them goof off. Or what kind of teacher says it's okay for the student not to study? They push them, asking them to broaden their minds and read, learn, and question, more and more. God wants the same for us...to be perfect...to be more like Him...so He will push us...and life will be difficult...but if we persevere, we will be tenaciously strong:

- *"My son, do not despise the chastening of the Lord, Nor be discouraged when you are rebuked by Him; For whom the Lord loves He chastens, And scourges every son whom He receives,"* (Hebrews 12:6).

- *"My brethren, count it all joy when you fall into various trials, knowing that the testing of your faith produces patience. But let patience have its perfect work, that you may be perfect and complete, lacking nothing. If any of you lacks wisdom, let him ask of God, who gives to all liberally and without reproach, and it will be given to him,"* (James 1:2-5).

- *"And not only that, but we also glory in tribulations, knowing that tribulation produces perseverance; and perseverance, character; and character, hope,"* (Romans 5:3-4).

Because life is difficult and Satan wants to take us down, we need to help each other out! This can't happen if we compare ourselves to each other and settle for being "better than" another person. Though I joked about a 300-pound glutton earlier in this chapter, this is an easy but unfair target. It's easy to pick on fat people because you can SEE they're fat. The same goes for a stumbling drunk. You can see or smell his sin and label him as a boozer or bum. However, God is far more concerned about impatient, arrogant or envious people. But these people aren't publicly slandered because they are more behind-the-scene sins. Exercising too much or eating too little can be as equally sinful as eating too much. If you're in the gym so much that you're not able to financially provide for your family, that's wrong. Your family is paying a hard price because of your vanity. And eating too little is a vain pursuit so that you can have that "perfect body."

The Bible speaks plenty against vain people, just as it talks about gluttons and drunks. In fact, Solomon who was given just about anything he wanted, ruined himself through this vanity and even began Ecclesiastes with the phrase *"...vanity of vanities! All is vanity."* Even though he was wise, wealthy, and healthy, he was miserably unhappy. If

91

you read the rest of Ecclesiastes you would find him griping and complaining about life. It's sad. He had it all and is whining. I think that Ecclesiastes is in the Bible partly to show that even if God gives you everything, unless you do something positive with it, you are going to be a miserable old fool in the end. "Those damn kids," you'll say through your toothless mouth as you wave a stick at them. The point is that we all have things we need to improve and should get on about doing just that. If you need help, get help! In fact, Christians should have a network of true believers with myriads of talents to assist and help each other when necessary. I'm not saying this doesn't happen, but it's too rare and sporadic. If someone is skilled at making money, go for it and make a bunch so you can help when someone is in need financially. If another is caring enough to help someone's emotional needs, fill in when you see depression and sorrow. If you're a comedian, use it to build people up making them laugh. If you're an artist… well, um, you probably need to see the financial guy...

Christians need to be much more open and vulnerable instead of hiding behind the false veneer of "everything is just peachy." It is extremely rare that I meet people where everything is peachy. In fact, after talking to the "peachy people," they are often the ones you find are the best at covering up a crappy life! The reality is, life is a balancing act. Be real about your life and don't be fake-happy when you're really secretly depressed and cursing God. Find ways to be thankful to God. We have to stop pretending, stop gossiping, and get on building a truly loving community where we can help the hurting and build each other up. Only then will those on the outside want in.

In conclusion, Christians, we need to seek God first rather than continuing to live for our own desires and playing by our own rules, thereby making a fool out of ourselves and mocking God. As we draw closer to God, we will more clearly see His goals rather than our own, and begin to understand the essence of God: Who He is and how He works with us. God is all-knowing and all-seeing. He knows the tiny intricacies of how our brains work and what we are thinking, but He doesn't change our brains to force us into His ways. He gives us free will and allows us to see His better way to change ourselves. He says he will comfort us in times of need, but he's not going to coddle us when we throw ourselves on the ground in a hissy fit. He requires a relationship. He is not a puppeteer. If he were, he would not have given us the choice to tell him to screw off. Instead, God lovingly allows us to *choose* Him. To choose to follow His ways. And what is the number one thing that God wants from us when we choose Him? To love Him and love others, (Mark 12:28-31). How effectively are we carrying this out? Currently, people inside and outside the church are jumping ship faster than rats with a legion of cats on board.

Jesus said Christians would be persecuted like he was, but still if we were doing our "love" job better, people would be banging on our doors to join our community. Christians, like it or not, it is us the world looks to when considering if this God of Jesus is real. If we are not representing Him correctly, we are in effect chasing them from the truth. This should change us! If we claim to love God, we need to be different- Christ died for us! Let's be in this game of life together and start loving others as God loves them- no matter their religion, beliefs, or differences. Here's a story to encourage and challenge you to love others and represent God well:

Two stylish Muslim brothers confidently entered my coin shop. They were in town from their native country, Kuwait, supporting their father who was recovering from surgery. They were overtly friendly and spoke better English than I do. They were extraordinarily likable and we quickly engaged on a personal level. A friendship was born. As with anyone who enters our store, I have no agenda. That's right Christians, my intent is never to *force* my opinion on people. I let God take control of that. I will speak on whatever subject is presented, with no effort to control or twist it into a sermon. After all, God says love "does not insist on its own way." I trust God, and HE miraculously presents unforced opportunities to lovingly talk about His truth.

Among numerous subjects discussed that morning I asked my new friends if they were devout Muslims, to which they quickly and enthusiastically answered, "Yes!" "Awesome" I said, "I am a devout follower of Christ and look forward to your perspective on life and what the Qur'an has to say about it." (Now don't be put off Christians, read on). We verbally explored life together all the while I asked what the Qur'an had to say about it. No agenda, just curious and I'm always trying to learn. They were knowledgeable and very willing to share Allah's word. I respected the devotion to their faith. We did fair business at the shop and they came back several more times, each time digging deeper into previous subjects. For the first couple visits, neither my God nor the Bible were discussed, and if they had never come up that would have been fine. God loves them more than I do and He will present Himself as He wants.

Our friendship deepened. I can't recall what we were discussing but a subject came up that allowed me to share my passion of discussing God's definition of love. It seemed to make an impression on both of them. The older brother addressed this "love" just shortly before returning to Kuwait. He said words very close to: "Something you said really made me think," as he tapped his heart with his hand instead of his head, (which I found to be a curious gesture since it would seem that you would tap your head if something made you think). "I will never forget your words on love. I am taking it back home with me to be more patient and kind to my wife, children, family and friends." He was taking a major part of my God back home with him in his heart. God's truth and seeds were planted. (There are those who plant, those who water, and those who reap [John 4:37]). This shows the true character of this man.

He heard what he perceived as truth and promised to employ it, rather than just talk about it. Christians, we need to take a lesson from this man in *acting* on what we know to be the truth- not just hearing and doing nothing.

The brothers' devotion was very real. When it came the hour for his time of prayer one brother courteously asked if he could pray to Allah in the store or should he leave to pray and come back. Since we have a private section in our store I said he could pray in the store and he asked me about directions so he could face Mecca. (Again, Christians read on). While he did this, I prayed that my God would be revealed to him. Kathy, a lovely older lady on fire for the Lord, came into the store and I told her of the Muslim brothers next door. She has a grassroots way of learning about God and always tells her husband and friends she's going to church when she comes to our store. While telling her about my experience with these gentlemen, I began to see how God may have been using me for His purpose. You see, over time as I was asking about the Qur'an, the brothers courteously started asking me about the Bible. I told Kathy that it gave me the chance to talk about the truth because the *true* God's Word does not come back void, (Isaiah 55:11). The truth will shine through, which is why I have no fear in talking about or reading other "religious" books. Any book other than God's Holy Word are vapid.

Many other topics were discussed in a direct, non-fluffy way. At one point we even both acknowledged wanting each other to convert to our professed religion. The other brother came in twice more. The second to last visit he presented me with a gift of which he had purchased two. It was a replica of a Kuwaiti Boom sailing ship. He gave one to his now recovered father and, humbly, one to me. That special gift is proudly displayed on a center shelf in our store. Towards the end of their stay in Pittsburgh, my Muslim friends brought their now recovered father to our shop. I considered this an honor. He is a gregarious man of goodwill and upbeat nature. It's no wonder his sons were so remarkable.

6

My Answer is No

I love my son-in-law Alexander. He came from quality stock-loving parents who clearly nurtured him into the man I saw. But this didn't stop me from picking on him many times, (with many more to follow I suspect). My daughter, Alexandra (yes, yes, Alexander and Alexandra...) had been dating Alex for about three years, and I knew the fateful day of my daughter permanently leaving was nigh. Twenty-one years (7,789 days not including leap years,) of raising and enjoying my daughter was coming to an end. Like "I Dream of Jeannie," I tried to blink her back to age four but it didn't work. "OK, OK," I said to myself. "You knew this day was coming. Breathe....breeeathe..." "Yeah, but how did it come so fast?!" I counter-argued. Then I remembered the words from the *Fiddler on the Roof* musical in which Alexandra had a key role in high school. "Sunrise, sunset, quickly go the days..." Panic. Well if my daughter is going to hook up with some DUDE, (even though I love him,) I'm not gonna make it easy for him. The fateful day came. "Dad..." said Alexander, (he has two awesome dads- God and Chuck, but he also wanted to call me dad,) "...Can we go out to breakfast? I'd like to ask you something." I tried to pretend he didn't say anything by plugging my ears and saying "Nanananananananananananahhhhhhh" really fast and loud. It didn't work; Alex persisted. I was ready, I just didn't want to be. "Oh man, it's really happening..."

Unbeknownst to me, Alexandra warned Alex this wasn't going to be easy. We went to Denny's. Alex was all smiles, I was the opposite. I started by gruffly asking, "Why are we here?" I purposely set a serious tone. Still smiling he said, "Oh okay, you want me to get right to it. Well, I would like to ask for your daughter's hand in marriage." "Is that a serious question?" I shot back. With a slightly confused look he said, "Yes." ... "My answer is no." After a short, uncomfortable few seconds he politely asked, "Are you serious?" I said, "Yes". His smile was gone, replaced now with full confusion. "I don't know what to do or say now," he stated. I said, "You know I like you, right?" He said, "Well yeah, I thought you did…" "It's not my job or desire to give my daughter away. It's her job to leave me and my protection for you." I wanted him to realize the importance of the new "position" for which he was asking and to show him exactly how God's Word put it. *A child shall LEAVE…* (Matthew 19:4-6). No way am I going to GIVE her away," I said. "Let me ask you a question. If I had a pound of pure gold sitting on my coffee table for all the years you were coming to my house, and at the end of those years you said, 'Can I have the gold?' what do you think I would say?" Alex replied, "You would say no." "How much more precious do you think my daughter is than that gold?" Alex, being the sharp guy that he is, got it at that point. As a dad, I was putting him on notice that if he was replacing me, then I wanted him to see my daughter in the same light: more precious than gold. I also wanted him to see that God's Word was more important than mine. Don't get me wrong, Alex was doing an age-old, noble thing by caring enough to ask me, and I appreciated it, but I wanted to make an impression that he would remember. The rest of the Denny's breakfast was jovial and upbeat, but for Alex it was about to get even more odd.

Even though I wasn't told directly that Alex and Alex were planning marriage, it was pretty clear that they were a special team and it was going to happen. I don't like to be caught flat-footed on matters of life, or knowing how God's Word answers life's questions. God asks us to have a ready answer to defend our faith (1 Peter 3:15-16). So, I thought it would be right to study marriage from a biblical perspective in order to most accurately share God's Word on the subject. What I found, or more accurately *didn't* find in the Bible, was that the traditional marriage in which so many Christians participate, is mainly made up. As a result, my perspective on marriage RADICALLY changed. This was shocking, but great! It woke me up to the reality that many traditions in the church are just that: traditions, and they are man-made rather than God-said. "Wow, I have a lot more learning to do," I thought. This is one huge reason each of us should study the Bible on our own instead of *only* listening to someone else's opinion. Pastors, ministers, bishops, et al, are just people with opinions and interpretations. They didn't author the Bible and are trying to learn from it like every other Christian should be. If these heads of church were perfect and could perfectly interpret God's Word, then there would be only one denomination - Christian. But there are thousands or tens of thousands of denominations because we are always splitting over differences in interpretation. When someone says, "My pastor says..." I often want to quip back, "So?"

"But, but, they went to hoity toity divinity school!"
"...So?"

I ask Christians what THEY think and most often they say they haven't studied the Bible, let alone even bothered reading it. WHY?! You are believing in something you don't know, can't explain, have never read, and allowing some stranger, (with their own baggage) to interpret for you?! No wonder non-Christians think we're lame! Christians must do better and step up their game to read and study God's Word. It's not acceptable *just* to believe. The Bible says in James 2:14, *"What good is it, my brothers, if someone says he has faith but does not have works? Can that faith save him?"* And in verse 19 it says, *"You believe that God is one; you do well. Even the demons believe-and shudder."* It's not just a mind belief. It takes a heart conversion. The Bible puts it both ways by saying to seek God with all your heart, MIND, soul and STRENGTH, (Luke 10:27). God clearly wants us to use our minds as part of accepting His truth into our souls. So, belief in the true God is decidedly not just blind faith, as atheists and "intellectuals" falsely state. They lie to themselves and the world by saying that Christians blindly believe in a myth instead of seeing there are facts and provable completed prophecies.

 I was so stunned by the research of the Bible on the marriage subject, I thought I must be missing something and needed to look deeper into the definitions of the original Greek and Hebrew words. I came away even more convinced of my position. Most of the "moral" commands in the Bible are clear. We may have a problem on agreeing with or doing them, but it's not complicated to understand things like, *"Thou shall not commit murder,"* or *"Love is patient."* We don't read these commands and say, "I wonder what those mean." They're obvious! So the definition of marriage was equally simple and clear.

 God defined marriage right after He created Eve in Genesis 2:24, *"Therefore a man shall leave his father and his mother and hold fast, (cleave), to his wife, and they shall become one flesh. And the man and wife were both naked and were not ashamed."* PLEASE take note, prudish Christians, "They were NAKED and NOT ASHAMED!" God is not a prude. He created our nakedness, including the plumbing, and said it was good, (Genesis 1:31.) In fact, He had every intention of us being nudists forever. It was only after Adam and Eve sinned that they even noticed they were naked and God (knowing full well) said, *"Who told you that you were naked?"* (Genesis 3:11). By disregarding God's words, their embarrassment of nakedness was a sin because in the previous verse it says Adam heard the sound of God in the garden and was afraid BECAUSE he was naked, so he hid himself. The naked body is created by a non-prudish, loving God for the pleasure of each other, but within His guidelines. And no, non-Christians, it is not anything goes, anywhere, any way, with anyone. It is not okay to have sex with a goat or your neighbor's wife, (Leviticus 18:33, 18:20). Can you imagine how ridiculous the scenario with Adam hiding his dangly from God was?

God: "Adam?"

Adam: "I'm hiding."

God: (Thinking to himself, "Yeah, I know.") says, "Why?"

Adam: "I'm naked."

God: (Thinking to himself, "Yeah, I know") says, "Who told you?"

God knew everything, but was forcing Adam to admit his sin. God could have just as easily told Adam He knew he was naked, He knew where he was hiding and He knew he had a dangly because He created it. But yet, there's Adam over in the reeds, legs crossed, hands over his unmentionables, as if God hadn't ever seen him naked.

You see, non-Christians, God isn't the prude. His people are. But once sin and embarrassment entered the world, God lovingly made Adam and Eve clothes, (Genesis 3:21). (There's no finer tailor in the world, I might add.)

In the New Testament, Matthew 19:5, Jesus defines marriage the same way as in Genesis, but adds a line in verse 6, *"So they were no longer two, but one flesh. What therefore GOD joined together, let no man separate."* There is no other definition of marriage in the Bible. For the sake of boring the reader, I will place in the back of the book an email exchange I had with a highly intelligent, honorable Christian, outlining the research I did to come to my reversal on thinking what Godly marriage is. Now let's look deeper at God's definition of marriage. It involves a man and woman. They choose to leave the protection of the parents, and cleave to each other, BECOMING ONE FLESH. What God united, let no one separate. It can't be any simpler. God created sex for marriage, fun, and procreation. He created the plumbing and fully understands its functionality. There is no *biblical* evidence of a priest, minister, et al marrying anyone. They have NO business in the marriage of two people. They have no GODLY right in stating, "I now pronounce you man and wife." In fact, the church got this authority from the *State* rather than from God. God sanctions marriages, not man!

I get angry at Christians when they berate homosexuals for redefining marriage. Gays did not hijack marriage, Christians did! Gays just went along with a system set up by the State that Christians agreed to. Again, if we paid attention to God and His Word rather than people's traditions, this wouldn't even be an issue. Yet Christians go about wringing their hands and saying marriage is has been hijacked.

If we were to take God at His Word that marriage is the consummation of the sexual union between a man and woman under His authority, it would radically change a substantial amount of things for Christians:

- 1) People (believers) would/should take VERY seriously having "premarital" sex, IF they believed that having sex was the actual marriage. "Premarital" sex in the church is a very serious problem. Why? No consequences. If the Church started preaching that the sexual union was marriage as God's Word states, wouldn't more people curtail that behavior until they found the person they wanted to marry? In fact, there is no such thing as premarital sex. The agreed union of a man's and woman's bodies IS marriage- leave and cleave- THE TWO BECOME ONE.

- 2) The "problems" today with "homosexual marriage" would not even exist if we just paid attention to God's simple definition of marriage. It says the male and female choose to leave and cleave, and what God put together let no one separate. If the church did not add to these verses to include having pastors (or the state) give the okay, then there could not be any homosexual marriage. God clearly states the MALE and FEMALE unite. But now homosexuals have a valid point claiming marriage rights because of the licensing and sanctioning process of the secular state that the church has willingly subjected itself to!

- 3) Non-Christians would see Christians giving God the recognition for His invention of sex and giving Him all the glory for uniting the husband and wife. *"...what God put together (let no man separate)..."* This is very important because it puts the attention back on God rather than an over-the-top sanctimonious ceremony or on pastors who initiate unbiblical decrees, "I now pronounce you man and wife," or, "You may now kiss the bride," or "By the powers vested in me by the state of Pennsylvania…"

- 4) Divorces would be significantly reduced because people would know they are making a promise to God in their sexual union and not to people- "What GOD put together…". Christians should know that lying to God is a really bad idea and may think twice or thrice before entering this sexual marriage.

Shortly after the shock of this marriage "revelation," I was oking with my adult niece that the wedding ceremony should be without a church overseer (pastor) and the couple should say in front of all nvited, "We had sex last night and it was great!" Then those invited would burst out in applause. Can you imagine the reaction of non-Christians in the audience? Our great God would be heralded for the entire ceremony and be shown in a dramatic way that He is no prude. It is from this sexual union, not "I do" union that a husband and wife are bound to each other as long as they live. We unwittingly take for granted that God created sex and if we were more appreciative we hopefully would pay more attention to all the other roles and guidelines on marriage that He suggests.

Since we have ignored God's marriage definitions and roles, marriage is in tatters. Unfortunately the church has been complicit in marriages destruction. I could write an entire spin-off book of this subject and perhaps will. I am awed by Satan's success **in first** leading Christians away from God's clear definition of marriage, then despicably embracing the world's definition. Then Christians added their own thoughts and traditions muddying God's definition. Sex then becomes an "inconsequential" recreation, but leaves scars. **Because we no longer accept God's parameters of marriage, ultimately we have inadvertently accepted** anything. Marriage is so bastardized that it no longer has a real definition. So then we have people who legally want to marry their pets or even their computer.

Because Christians are part of this anything- goes marriage, we don't pay much attention to His other decrees about marriage roles. God's Word says a wife is bound to her husband as long as he lives, (1 Corinthians 7:39). If this is true, then we have stepped far past those words. Statistics suggest that women sue for divorce in about seventy percent of marriages. Today, marriage seems more like a testing ground than a commitment. We even have a commercial campaign advertising, *"Life's short, have an affair."* We have lyrics to songs like Shania Twain's, "Any Man of Mine"[1] that says:

...I can be late for a date that's fine, But he better be on time.

…Any man of mine better walk the line.

…I need a man who knows, how the story goes.

…When I cook him dinner and I burn it black he better say, "Mmm, I like it like that."

…If I change my mind a million times I wanna hear him say, "Yeah, yeah, yeah, yeah, I like it that way."

…This is what a woman wants…

If this is what women want, no wonder that guy wants to marry his computer.

As Christians lamentably ignore God's Word on marriage, we try our own hand at explaining it through writing tons of books on the subject. Are they all wrong? Well I don't know, I haven't read them all, but most probably are. I have read many, and all but one of them was biblically distorted. They may have the *essence* of God's words on marriage, but then deviate into the author's own definition. Marriage is now defined by the individual rather than God. It's no wonder people are confused.

Okay, back to Alex and the rest of our marriage conversation at breakfast. Alexandra and Alex were still both virgins and believed in abstaining from sex to be pure for each other on their wedding day. I told Alex after studying the Bible for God's description of marriage that if he and my Alexandra truly intended to marry, they should go have sex together and I would pay for the marriage/honeymoon location. The blank stare I got back from him was priceless. "You're telling me to have sex with your daughter?!" "Yep, and I'll pay for the location. Go unite yourselves under God's authority and have fun. Do it before the wedding ceremony so you can tell all of your invited guests about the wonderful God we serve."

After breakfast, Alex went back to my daughter who previously warned him that talking to me that morning was not going to be normal or easy. She asked him how it went and he said, "You were right on both accounts. It wasn't easy or normal. He said we should have sex." My daughter was as amused as he was. However, out of respect for Alex's parents and the tradition they believe in, they waited until after the "I do's". Ironically, the niece I was joking with about how a real Christian ceremony should go, DID marry this way. They dedicated their bodies to each other before their Creator and THEN had the wedding ceremony. Christians, before saying that I'm wrong, please read the entire study and conversation at the back of the book. Your traditions are fine unless they detract or alter God's Word.

Since I had searched the Bible on the marriage subject, Alex and Alexandra asked me to write their wedding vows. Because I believe God's Word has the answer for marriage and the husband and wife roles, then His Word alone would suffice. Posted below is what I compiled. After spending weeks completing the vows, I read them straight through and was overwhelmed to the point of tears at the beauty of God's Word in defining the interactions and importance of our roles. If husbands and wives were to fulfill their duties with and for each other, we would have solid, meaningful marriages and strong families. Shortly after writing the vows I took it to my Bible study that had several men and one married couple. I wanted to see if it had the same impact on others as it did on me. I asked the couple if they would read them to each other as if they were just getting married. They teared up half way through and could barely finish reading them to each other. Here they are:

(Man) I, Alex, promise by the sweat of my brow to work hard and provide for our well being, (Genesis 3:19).

(Woman) I, Alexandra, will be your helper and partner, (Genesis

106

2:18).

(Man) I see you as far more precious than jewels because my heart trusts in you. I will rise up in the morning and praise you saying "You surpass all women," (Proverbs 31: 10-1).

(Woman) I promise to bring you good and not harm all the days of my life. To provide for my family. To open my mouth with wisdom and the teaching of kindness on my tongue (Proverbs 31:10-31).

(Man) I will continue to learn of my awesome responsibility to be the head of this union just as Christ is the head of me, being made in the image of God, (1 Corinthians 11:3-12).

I promise to love you, Alexandra and never treat you harshly, (Colossians 3:19).

(Woman) I know that I was created for you and that I will be dependent upon you as you will be dependent upon me, (1 Corinthians 11: 9-12).

(Man) As we live as husband and wife, I will be considerate, treating you with honor as the weaker vessel and be heirs together of the gracious gift of life so that our prayers will not be hindered, (1 Peter 3:7).

(Woman) I will submit myself to you, for this is fitting in the Lord, (Colossians 3:18), (Ephesians 5:21-24).

(Man) I need to understand that my duty as a husband and a man is to be self- controlled, in all respects a model of good works, and in my teaching to show integrity, seriousness and soundness of speech that cannot be condemned so that even my enemies will have nothing evil to say of us, (Titus 2:1-8).

(Woman) I need to understand that my duty as a wife and a woman is to be reverent in behavior, not a slanderer or slave to drink, but to encourage women to love their husbands, to love their children, to be self controlled, chaste, good managers of the household, kind, being submissive to their husbands, so that the Word of God may not be blasphemed, (Titus 2:3-5).

(Man) I am awestruck at my position that I need to be subject to you out of reverence for Christ, loving you as Christ loved the church giving himself up for her. Knowing I must nourish and tenderly care for you as I would myself just as Jesus does for the church. For this reason I am choosing to leave my father and mother and join with you in this holy and mysterious event, (Ephesians 5:21-33).

(Woman) I accept the authority of my husband, adorning my inner self with the lasting beauty of a gentle and quiet spirit, for this is very precious in God's sight, (1 Peter 3:1-6).

(Man) Alexandra...
I choose you...
to be my wife. The two of us becoming one.
I desire to love you. To be patient and kind with you. I will not be envious, boastful or arrogant. I will not insist on my own way be resentful or irritable. I will rejoice in truth and not in wrongdoing. I will bear all, believe all, hope all and endure all.

My love for you will never end, (1 Corinthians 13:4-8).

(Woman) Alex...
I choose you...
to be my husband. The two of us becoming one.
I desire to love you. To be patient and kind with you. I will not
be envious, boastful or arrogant. I will not insist on my own way,
be resentful or irritable. I will rejoice in truth and not in
wrongdoing. I will bear all, believe all, hope all and endure all.
My love for you will never end, (1 Corinthians 13:4-8).

7

Spread **** on their Face (Malachi 2:3)

Christians, would you have been offended at this chapter title if I didn't put the verse next to it? Be honest. I bet you wouldn't have thought it was in the Bible. So, let's get this out in the open now. I am likely to offend you dainty- eared Christians where, at the whisper of a "swear" word, a trickle of blood may be seen coming from your ears as you scream, "NAUGHTY NAUGHTY!" But, Christians, PLEASE understand that if you are focused so much on a word, your focus is NOT on loving the person using it!

The world is harsh. In many places and many ways, very harsh, where even daily survival is difficult. Every day, we are bombarded with inhuman savagery so barbaric it's nearly impossible to comprehend. The list of horrors the world experiences every day would fill a tome; torture, murder, slavery, pedophilia, rape, terrorism, starvation, poverty, wrongful severe anger, impatience, slander, lies, cheating, arrogance. These are crimes committed against others, but we commit heartbreaking crimes against ourselves as well; suicide, overindulging on drugs, alcohol and food, overspending, divorce, betrayal, bragging, vanity, arrogance, selfishness, envy, and laziness. Then there are illnesses resulting from a fallen world like cancer and all other unfortunate diseases that people unfairly contract. If every aspect of all of life's problems were written down, *swearing* would not, or perhaps should not, even be mentioned in the book.

Christians, are you offended by these words- kak, mut, pox, kaka, sranje, merda, zoyipa, mmerda, hovno, lort, stront, merdo, sitt, tae, paska, merde, Scheisse, szar, skit, na na, kotoran, cac, telek, stercore, sudi, sudas, schsiss, diky, najis, dritt, gowno, rahat, fhalbh, robho, shire, mierda, bok, di tieu, cachu, ikaka, nik? These words are from Google translate and if they don't offend you, then neither should the word "shit" since that's what all those words mean from languages around the world. I especially like "fhalbh" which is Scottish or Gaelic for "shit." You see, "fhalbh" looks and sounds nonsensical or funny to most of the world. Perhaps a teeny-tiny populace of the world may find it offensive since there are approximately 58,000 Scottish Gaelic souls on earth putting the overall possible offendees at .000008 percent. But then we must account for the children who are too young to know or understand fhalbh, lowering further the offendees' numbers. Certainly, we can't forget about the beer guzzling, truck driving, hard nose brawlers of Scottish Gaelic descent who may potentially use fhalbh as a replacement word for ANY noun or adjective. So, the offendees' numbers must be lowered again. Then there are those whom the word may not really even bother. And WAIT! What about the farmers who use the word in describing the, uh, stuff that comes out the, umm, rectal cavity of the farm animals? (I'm tip-toeing here, tip-toeing, don't want to offend the dainty-eared). Now one may say the farmer would describe such farm animal deposits as manure, which is just a sanitized word for the "naughty" word describing the unsanitary by-product. But is manure any better? Why doesn't this word offend? Or does it? How about poop, crap or dung? Is that okay? So, after re-calculating, it's possible that only .000003 percent of the world's population MIGHT be offended by the word "fhalbh." I think Christians should rise up and protest fhalbh- because a word is so much more important than someone's soul. Obviously, I'm being absurd in part to show that words are social norms and offend for that reason, not for the word itself. For those that may even get offended by the word "manure," you may want to bury your head when coming across these biblical verses:

- *"But the flesh of the bullock, and his skin, and his ****, shalt thou burn with fire without the camp: it is a sin offering,"* (Exodus 29:14).

- *"And thou shalt eat it as barley cakes, and thou shalt bake it with **** that cometh out of man, in their sight,"* (Ezekiel 4:12).

- *"Yea doubtless, and I count all things but loss for the excellency of the knowledge of Christ Jesus my Lord: for whom I have suffered the loss of all things, and do count them but ****, that I may win Christ,"* (Philippians 3:8).

- *"Behold, I will corrupt your seed, and spread **** upon your faces, even the **** of your solemn feasts; and one shall take you away with it,"* (Malachi 2:3).

For cryin' out loud, look at the Malachi 2:3 verse talking about putting poop on people's faces and food! Don't blast me though for pointing this out, I'm just the messenger of God's message.

If that's not enough, here are several other verses saying similar things: Job 20:7, Psalm 83:10, Jeremiah 16:4, Zephaniah 1:17, Luke 13:8, and Luke 14:35.

If these verses do not make the point of naughty words being in the Bible, here's more:

- *"But Rabshakeh said unto them, 'Hath my master sent me to thy master, and to thee, to speak these words? Hath he not sent me to the men which sit on the wall, that they may eat their own dung, and drink their own piss with you?'"* (2 Kings 18:27).

- *"But was rebuked for his iniquity: the dumb ass speaking with man's voice forbad the madness of the prophet,"* (2 Peter 2:16).

- *"And a bastard shall dwell in Ashdod, and I will cut off the pride of the Philistines,"* (Zechariah 9:6).

Since God used these harsh words, it's clear the words aren't wrong, and in some cases, are useful. If not, God would not have used them. Often it is the context, manner, and frequency in which words are used, (as George Carlin will explain in a bit). If someone were to angrily and loudly blurt out curse words in a fancy restaurant, such as, "This food looks like s**t!", it would be offensive and inappropriate. However, if a farmer used the *same word* when answering a city dude about what the raisin- looking things on the ground around the rabbit hutch are, it would seem to be a reasonable answer. We should all courteously take into consideration our environment and whether the context is appropriate.

Again, I believe this whole "life" thing comes down to love- we should all be keeping each other in mind instead of insisting on our own way. If someone uses words that you choose not to, don't judge and discount the person using them. You may not like the words, but at least have the decency to LISTEN to their thoughts. And, if you are one who uses swear words, but the context is clearly inappropriate, don't blurt them out just because you can! I had this personal example years ago with my kids:

Several years ago, my family went on vacation to Disney. One of the days, Epcot was on the agenda, and though my wife was too tired to go, our five kids and I still decided to go. After spending a rambunctious day on the rides and outdoor activities, we decided to eat at a nicer sit-down restaurant, the fancy Chinese one. After entering and being asked, "How many?" and I said "Six," I could see the host silently count... one dad, and... one... two... three... four... five... young kids. He frowned and placed us as far away from everyone as he possibly could. If I recall right, he set up a card table in the back alley next to the trash bins.

I wasn't upset because I knew he was responding from past experiences of unacceptable parents inadequately trying to control unruly kids... normally it doesn't go well. You never know what is going to come out of a kid's mouth. We had a wonderful meal and discussion. The waiter complimented me on parenting but several others came up to me and told me how "lucky" I was to have such well-behaved kids. As any parent can tell you, "luck" rarely plays a part in raising good kids. The optimal word is similar because it starts with an "L" and is also four letters long- love. I explained to each of these luck-commenters that my kids are super athletic with lots of energy to dissipate *in the proper venue*. Inside a restaurant is not one of those places. Acting loud, whining, speaking inappropriately, and running around in a restaurant is disrespectful. Doing the exact same thing in a field is not. So, just like appropriate kids' behavior in a restaurant, swearing can be acceptable depending on the context. Again, if you think it isn't, then why did God use them in the Bible?

So, swearing to express pain or frustration, or swearing because it's the norm of the culture you grew up in, may not be wrong or inappropriate. However, swearing loud and obnoxiously without giving a damn about others around you is wrong because you are choosing not to love- Love says it is not rude or arrogant, and when you act that way, you *are* rude and arrogant. So, it's really not about the words you're using, it's the context and attitude in which you use them.

Ok, back to naughty words.

If I were retelling an actual story of a huge man who entered my store, pointed a gun at my head, and *literally* said, "Do as I say or I will blow your fucking head off," should I sensor that speech to you Christians? If so, why? If so, how? Should I say the man said, "I'm going to blow your 'faithful' head off?" Well no, that would be a lie. Should I put the cartoony symbols in its place like this: @#%*! ? What about suggesting the word but not fully spelling it out like this: f**king. Or how about blurring the middle or perhaps spelling it "phuque"? Is that better? Also, since I spelled the naughty word, "phuque," and the reader said in his head "f**k," is he now complicit in a thought sin or am I wrong for "forcing" him to think dirty?

It just seems so fucking pretentious and pious to the point of ridiculousness in pretending that this is not how real life is. Oh, I'm sorry, did I say fucking pretentious? I guess I should have said f**king pretentious. Christians, you may find the words vulgar, but comparatively, it's hardly worth getting your knickers in a wad, (or is saying that offensive too?). Most of these words are exclamations, or non-descriptive adjectives, which have virtually no meaning. If someone said "...it was fuckin hilarious," it means it was really funny, not anything more or less. If you don't want to use the words... DON'T! Admittedly, when people use these words too much, they sound dumb. I had a customer who said fuck every other word. This was hardly an exaggeration and he sounded ridiculous, but I still listened to his *every other word* while trying to make sense of what he was saying.

So, Christians, stop trying to control people and their language. If you cared more about these people and loving them as God has asked us to, rather than their "uncouth" words, people might actually be willing to listen to you. They might not so readily agree that Christians "suck" because of our piety and judgmentalism towards a silly word. Judgmentalism is a complaint I often hear from non-Christians towards Christians. They are tired of being told what to do, how they're wrong and that their words are naughty. For example, I had a **very bright,** lovely young lady come into our store one day, and of course, we started talking. She was severely abused as a child and unfortunately is now addicted to life-destroying, harsh drugs to cover the pain. She said, "I wish people would stop 'shoulding' all over me." If it's not clear, she was cleverly equating and using "shoulding" in the place of "shitting". She continued, "...you know... everyone knows better than me and says 'you should…'" This is a woman who has lived through unspeakable pain, and yet, instead of listening to, and loving, her, people tell her what she should do. As if a swear word that she uses somehow is *worse* than her horrid experiences. Can you see how maddening this would be for her, and the millions like her? Right away you are signaling you don't care about her- you care about YOU and your piety. This is the very person that needs compassion through a listening ear, not condemnation by your closed mind.

Along this same theme, one morning about eight a.m., I was taking the trolley to work with two of my boys aged about ten and eight. There was a man on the other side of the tracks with half a case of beer, already drunk. Yes, he was... drunk. Many Christians scoff at people in this position saying basically it's their own fault and they need to just stop "sinning." Ultimately, they are right, but where's the love, grace or compassion? So even though I agree that we all need to take responsibility for ourselves at some point, these people who are in trouble and suffering need compassion, not condemnation at that point. There is a reason they are in that predicament. If you condemn a person in that condition of weakness, they likely will consume the other half of the case while they curse you under their breath. By condemning, you may inadvertently *aid* their drinking instead of possibly helping them take a step in God's direction. Not condemning them does not mean you are condoning their behavior, however.

So, I said to the fella in an upbeat tone, trying to start a dialog to reach his heart, "Dude, it looks like you got an early start!" He slurred something I couldn't understand, got up and staggered over to the three of us. He told me of his woes, which were many, all-the-while cursing up a storm. I got to see his eyeball up close, really up close, as he leaned to within a whisker of my face and pulled the skin below his eye, revealing the red interior. (I think I counted 14 freckles on his left cheek.) He told me about his cataracts and lack of funds to do anything about it, all the while continuing to curse. At some point, he slowly looked over at my wide- eyed boys and slurred, "I guess I shouldn't be swearing in front of your kids." I told him I was not the thought police or the word police and he could use any language he was comfortable with. I said my kids would ultimately make up their own minds about whether they wanted to use these words. You see, it's my responsibility to raise my kids by introducing them to this stuff and discussing it with them. It is not up to a drunk stranger to help raise my kids. The result was that the stranger was convicted on his own accord, my kids heard how dumb the words sounded, and saw that I was more compassionate about his soul rather than a word. This man's reality was harsh and he chose to cope with it through things like alcohol and swearing. Are we to condemn the pain he endures? In the end, if you are trying to control a person's words, where does that stop? What if the person is arrogant, rude, envious or impatient? Should you try and control those aspects of people too? Actually if Christians were being consistent with the Bible, they should condemn an impatient person before a drunk!

In addition to milk-toasty Christians who are quick to plug their ears upon hearing a swear word, secular society also has become quick to judge common words. Again, these are mere words!! Comedian George

Carlin hated religious people but also social justice pansies. In one of his bits he was talking about swear words and said:

> ...it's only words. It's the context that counts. It's the user. It's the intention behind the words that make them good or bad. Words are completely neutral. The words are innocent. I get tired of people talking about bad words and bad language. Bullshit. It's the context that makes them good or bad- they're only words. You can't be afraid of words that speak the truth even if it's an unpleasant truth like the fact that there's a bigot and a racist in every living room on every street corner of this country. I don't like words that hide the truth. I don't like words that conceal reality. I don't like euphemisms or euphemistic language and American English is loaded with euphemisms, cause Americans have a lot of trouble dealing with reality. Americans have trouble facing the truth, so they invent a kind of soft language to protect themselves from it and it gets worse with every generation. ...toilet paper became bathroom tissue... deaf have become hearing impaired... stupid has become minimally exceptional... die = pass away.

Carlin continued by saying;

> Jesus healed the "cripples": "There's no shame to that word unless we *attribute* shame to it. We don't have cripples in this world anymore, we have the physically challenged." I vaguely recall another comedian who was in a wheelchair say he hates it when people use "politically correct" words saying he is "vertically challenged." He said something like, "there is no 'challenge' at all. I can't stand." Carlin again mused, "...as if you change the name of the condition that the condition itself will change." (You can hear his whole routine on YouTube if you type in "George Carlin" and "euphemism."[1])

Just as Carlin suggested, I believe our society has disengaged from reality and become proficient in the art of egocentrism and personal entitlement. Instead of engaging genuine people in a realistic way by listening and conversing with them, people are quick to be offended and are easily triggered by nearly anything... but a word?! What happened to "sticks and stones"?! A mere suggestion of a person's *name* running for political office triggered college students to seek professional psychological help. They created "safe spaces," brought in therapy dogs, held group cries, postponed midterm tests and gave days off to cope. People are triggered by mere SUGGESTIONS, not ACTUAL problems. This unstable emotionality creates an extremely dangerous environment, especially with the aid of rapidly spreading disinformation or misinformation through social media. Americans' first amendment rights are not being *legislated* out of existence, they are being boo-hooed out of existence by temperamental moaners.

Everyday words are now becoming verboten: "elderly," "crazy," "fat," "short," "bald;" and "male" or "female," are offensive to "gender neutral" identifiers. "Homosexual" is now replaced with "same gender loving." And "American" is offensive since we are all citizens of the world... Think I'm making this up? It gets even crazier. Do you know that part of the definition of "literally" now is "virtually"? "Literally" was so often used in a figurative way by simpletons, (is that offensive or the truth?) that Merriam-Webster has redefined it by adding a meaning that is its *opposite*. Do your own research. This word obfuscation and manipulation is FAR worse than the few sentences imparted here. Before you know it, our entire lexicon will be changed to the point of a comedian Steve Martin's joke where he quips, "Wanna play a trick on your kid? ...Talk wrong whenever he's around so when he is in school he raises his hand and says to the teachers, 'May I mambo dog-face to the banana patch?'" Now that's a funny joke, but it's not funny when it is happening for real. It's even stepped into the non-word realm. Did you know clapping is frowned on now? That's right, you are supposed to air-shimmy your hands to show approval. But I'm sure this will eventually offend someone too. Soon we will all sit around saying nothing, with no expression, listening to nobody, being too afraid to say anything.

In a pure ironic twist, it is the people who once screamed "censorship", that are spearheading this ludicrousness. This new army of word police will even try to shut down opposing views by adding the suffixes of "-phobic" or "-ist" to the end of their made up, new, temporarily acceptable words. Whatever the offense-du-jour, just sprinkle in "phobia." So, if you have an alternative thought about homosexuality, you are now a homophobe. If you say anything about gender, you are a sexist. Say the word "black," even if it has no association to the color of skin and you are a racist. I recall when a media personality used the word niggardly- media went apoplectic. Because it *sounds* racist they assumed it was. These offense-takers are so ready to scream and slap a label on people that they now just react rather than think. The etymology of "niggard" is from either Old English or Norse that refers to a miser and has absolutely nothing to do with the "N" word. But logic doesn't seem to matter- only their vitriol and agenda matter.

Anyone can play this ridiculous suffix game, however. This has become so common. It is trite, boring and annoying- like a pesky mosquito that you can hear and keep trying to shoo away. So, now if someone wants to try and slap a label on you, have fun with it and slap one right back on them. If "they" call you a homophobe, xenophobe, islamophobe, etc., call them a logicphobe, fairnessphobe, Christosphobe, or Godphobe. You see, its easy. Whatever subject you disagree on, just say the other person is afraid of it by adding "phobe." Kids can play along too! It's fun for the whole family.

Though I jest, this problem of being easily offended by words has distracted us from what we *should* be doing- loving each other in patience and kindness. Instead of helping each other out, we judge each other's choice of words and choose to stay distant and offended. Let me ask you this- How do you respond to real words? Does vulva or penis offend you? What about "gosh" or "gee," which are just innocent expressions, right? In today's lexicon the words are laughably mild, but in the mid-18th century, it was euphemism for "God" and therefore seen at that time as taking the Lord's name in vain. At one point will we stop being offended? This goes for both Christians and non-Christians alike.

So, Christians, let's not play this game of instant-offense-taking because we disagree about witless words. The world sees Christians as petty when we **seem to** focus on things like this. And I would agree with the world on this matter. Let's love the people who use harsh words and ignore their ignoble vocabulary. You will never reach them if you demean their use of insignificant words without hearing their hearts.

8

Non-Christians... meh

"So, there is no God?"
"Nope."

Non-Christians, I bet you were quick to agree when I said in chapter one that I don't like Christians, and approved of the basic premise throughout this book that they suck. Well... you suck too.

BE FAIR and read the rest of this chapter otherwise you will be just as guilty of the same hypocrisy with which you label Christians. The brief opening conversation is one I've heard many times. Non-Christians are confident that there is no God, but based on what knowledge? Some people reject Jesus and the notion of God because they thought a bit about it. But, through my experiences, I've seen that the vast majority of people never engage their gray matter. They blissfully spend hours on social media talking about nothing, play zombie video games... like zombies, and memorize songs with unintelligible words as their minds surreptitiously go squishy. These sun-starved people are the ones that confidently say, "There is no God!" as they stuff their face with donuts and ponder weightier matters like clothing styles or the craziest memes.

There are deep thinking Christians that accept the truth of God because they have studied and researched, versus Christians who have blindly accepted Jesus because they grew up in the church and were told to. Non-Christians, *you are the same.* Some people after examining life have rejected God, however, most rely on someone else's opinion instead of *personally* studying the evidence. Maybe your parents were atheists and you blindly accepted their beliefs. Or maybe you didn't like your parents' "religion" and so went against it, only to never actually consider the truth of life.

Often, I have found that non-Christians don't want to put the effort into thinking and examining the evidence *for* God. It's far easier to make up your own rules and ways for living without ever engaging your hearts and your minds. Non-Christians, there are things that you believe or accept that don't really make sense. I want to challenge you to think throughout this chapter and take a look at why you do the things you do, or why you believe the things you believe.

As I said, sometimes we believe things just because someone else believes them, like our parents, teachers, friends, or perhaps we simply unconsciously accept societal norms. There are people who have embraced other religions based on the "evidence" they have been shown and those who also blindly accept it because they grew up in that culture. For example, the cultural norm in China may be to believe and accept Buddhism, as opposed to Hinduism in India or Islam in Indonesia. So, often when discussing religion, many people have said to me, "Well you know you would be a Muslim if you grew up in Indonesia, don't you?" To which I say, "Does that mean there could not be one *true* God?" Wherever you grow up, whatever religion you claim, doesn't negate the possibility of the one true God, it just shows how easy it is for people to be duped into believing **anything**. I can hear you chorus girls now saying, "Well maybe YOU'RE DUPED!" Maybe I am. Obviously, I think the God of Jesus does exist though, which is why I'm slogging through writing this book. I think believing in this true God is logically provable with a preponderance of the evidence.

The numerous religions of the world unfortunately establish that people create their own belief systems. There are four vastly different

124

"religions" that each have over 1 billion followers: Christianity, Islam, Non-religious (secular, atheist, agnostic) and Hinduism. "Religion" is just a term stating a system of beliefs. The term is really meaningless. When I'm asked if I'm religious, I say, "Yeah, I really like motorcycles and nature!" I believe they exist and are wonderful to participate in. I might've even made up my own religion based on those two things if I didn't believe in the God of Jesus. My motorcycle would be the altar upon which I sit as I rumble through nature and hear her sultry, sweet nothings breathlessly whispered in my ear;

"Brad", she would whisper... "Braaaaaad."
And I would quietly answer, "Yes, sweet nothings?"
"Do you love me?"
"Oh, I do! Let me count thy ways."

And there you have it! I just started a new religion. I would call it motor-nature or nature-cycle. See how simple it is! It can be fun for anyone- we can all pretend. (* See illustration on opposite page.)

In reality, this is how most religions start. We take an idea or thing and morph it into a deity and belief. **We worship the sun because it gives and sustains life, or all of nature because we are a living breathing part of it, or perhaps we worship our past ancestors believing they are watching over and protecting us.** We carve our own idol gods out of rock, give them a fancy name and pray to them. We make voodoo dolls. Sci-fi books are written and transmuted into religions. **The list of what people have placed their beliefs in is endless.** I laugh every time I see the "COEXIST" bumper stickers with all the religious symbols- as if all religions are equally valid. I want my new-found motorcycle religion added to that bumper sticker!

The number of people in a religion doesn't make it valid either. Just because Christianity is the largest religion and Islam is number two,

doesn't mean *either* are correct. It could mean they were able to dupe the most people. Hell, for all we know, Bubba in Toadvine, Alabama may be the only person on Earth that knows the one true God. We should all flock there and ask him.

The reality is, we are all trying to figure out why and how we exist. Some are putting more effort in than others. I applaud the ones searching. The people who say, "I DON'T GIVE A CRAP. I COULD CARE LESS WHY I EXIST," are the ones in *grave* danger. If God does exist, they are going to find out at the worst possible time… when they die. Just because you are too lazy to care about seeking the truth doesn't let you off the hook. I can see the sluggard's defense attorney at the pearly gates in heaven arguing his case:

"Listen, Mr. Jesus; may I call you that?"

"…"

"No?"

"…"

"It's disrespectful? How so?"

"…"

"Oh I see…you lived a tortured but perfect life and died for all mankind? I'm sorry… so, Messiah, my client here feels it's unfair for him to be locked out of heaven. He feels he was... uh… you know… basically a good man most of his life and he deserves better treatment. His argument is that you created him lazy so he really didn't have a choice to make the right decision. He demands a retrial AND an apology from you and your Father for his mental anguish and emotional distress. However, he is kindly declining any need for financial compensation. Just an apology will do."

"…"

"What's that?"

"…"

"Who created him? Well he feels nobody did."

"…"

"Then why's he here? … May I have a few moments to consult with my client? … He declines to answer the question on the grounds it may incriminate him."

"…"

"Excuse me?"

"…"

"Yes, that's correct, he never cared enough to see whether your claims were true."

"…"

"You heard him on Earth when he said he didn't give a crap

about you?"

"..."

"Oh, I see..."

Then the attorney turns to his client and says, "Yer screwed."

The whole point is, non-Christians, that life isn't a dress-rehearsal and you don't get to make up *your own rules or ignore God's.* When people don't feel like searching for truth, they ultimately just make up their own truths- what is right or wrong, what gives people value, what the meaning of life is, what they want God to do for them...

But, you see, God is not your personal, pink-tutu-wearing, dancing bear, that responds to your whip and demands. How ultimately arrogant are we as people to INSIST that God play by our rules? (*See image on opposite page.)

"I'm basically good and moral and it's insensitive to exclude me from heaven..."
"It's wrong that Christianity is so exclusionary..."
"What's wrong with a little lie. It's not hurting anyone..."
"It's unfair I can't make it into heaven just 'cause I didn't believe what he said..."
"It's not right that God's sets these parameters on marriage..."
"His rules are too complicated and oppressive..."

Do you see how dumb this sounds? But we do it all the time! I hear these arguments often. WE are TELLING God the laws and morals HE should adopt! It's insane and completely backwards! Atheists, if you peak about morals, unbeknownst to yourself, you are proving God's

129

Dancing Bear God

Word where it says that He has placed the knowledge of Himself, (His eternal nature), in all people, (Ecclesiastes 3:11 & 14). Most people know when they have done something "wrong." They know it inside; they *feel* it. Why? If we were just a bunch of pitiless cells dancing to our DNA as microbiologist, as atheist Richard Dawkins says, we would not feel this. If we are not getting our morals from the God who made us and placed eternity in our hearts, then where are you getting those *feelings* from? Where are your morals coming from? Are you getting them from popular rap artists who sings lyrics like, "Now if I f**k this model, And she just bleached her a**hole, And I get bleach on my T-shirt, I'mma feel like an a**hole." Or, how about learning the morals of life from this little ditty; "I don't like 'em figgity fat, I like 'em stiggity stacked/You wiggity wiggity wack if you ain't got biggish back." The second one is from an ordained minister (not kidding). Let's add one more from country music just for fun; "Got it goin' on like Donkey Kong and whoo-wee shut my mouth, slap your grandma there outta be a law get the sheriff on the phone lord have mercy, how's she even get them britches on that honky tonk badonkadonk, (Aww son)."

If you are not playing by God's rules, whose rules are you playing by? Regular people. The common Joe Schmo. I think it's more honorable to say, "I don't believe in God, so f**k you all, I'll do what I want, say what I want, and think what I want," rather than say, "I don't believe in God but I'm moral." Based on what?! Says who?! It's far more fair and logical to say there is either a rule book or there isn't. Can you imagine playing a sport by an arbitrary rule book? If a player didn't like some rules, he could add his own. You didn't like the fact that a running back made you look second-rate when he juked you? No problem, go up and punch him in the face. When you're flagged, punch the ref and tell him he's being oppressive and scream in his face that his rules are only meant to keep the little man down... then set his shirt on fire... and steal his wallet.

In fact, God's rule book should more accurately be called "His Guidelines or Suggestions." Sports are a dictatorship of restrictive, repressive rules. If you don't play by sports' rules, you can't play the game. If you're a really bad sport, you're thrown out of the stadium, *especially* if you offend the officials of the game. OHH NO, cross them and, "Yerrrrrr outta here!" Also, if you don't wear your protective gear, you can get hurt. In fact you're *demanded* to wear the proper equipment; if not, you sit for the whole game. YOU ARE NOT ALLOWED TO PLAY. God does not put such HARSH restrictions on us. He allows us to play the game of life without "proper" gear, without playing by the rules, and with ONLY a warning that you probably will get hurt. BUT… in the end… you will lose.

So we are perfectly willing to play by Joe Schmo's rules in a silly game, (sorry, sports lovers), but when it comes to God… naaaahh, we don't have to play by some oppressive celestial dictator's rules. WHO DOES HE THINK HE IS?!

Sports don't work without rules; neither does life. Ultimately the game would descend into chaos, just like life is now. Things are already strange but they will continue to get more and more strange as the world gets further and further away from God… until it will be difficult to differentiate between reality and insanity, (2 Timothy 3:3). You must get your mind and spirit right with God and His truth to be able to discern, (1 John 4:1-3).

The sports example is a simple analogy, but you can see that reasonable rules applied to a game makes the game enjoyable to watch and play. Contrarily, if it did descend into chaos, nobody except the lunatics would want to play. (However, it may be fun to watch). So, the sport rule book actually *frees* people to play a relevant game. God's rule book does the same. It frees you to live life and live it more abundantly, (John 10:10). He knows what's best for us. He would know, He made us! Ironically, most people even agree with the guidelines (morals) for life!

They just choose not to acknowledge where they came from. In fact, God calls His rule book the *"law of liberty"* which is one of my all-time favorite verses and makes my wannabe hippie heart happy, (James 1:25). This "law of liberty" is not forced or coerced; it's a choice. I love that. It's not long, confusing, and oppressive. However, it also doesn't mean we can do whatever we want, when we accept God's terms.

Because we have ignored God and His principles for so long, we don't know Him. He is not nearly as demanding as people imprudently suggest. As an example, He would like us to pray but doesn't tell us when, where, how long, how often, in what manner, or at what venue. He just says He likes it, so we should *want* to do it out of love, not force.

Unfortunately, sometimes I think Christians take this law of freedom almost as a license to sin because they believe they are saved and God will forgive whatever they do. These people also are in grave danger, just like the sluggard atheist. God says He will take a lukewarm Christian and chew him up and spit him out of His mouth, (Revelations 3:15-16). And on the last days when He is judging the world, God will tell many of those who claim to be Christians to get away from Him because He doesn't recognize them. This is in response to them praising Him with phony accolades as they lift their hands and cry out, *"Lord, Lord,"* (Matthew 7:21-23).

So, you see, God *wants* us to succeed in life- and He set us up for the possibilities of success by establishing the parameters for life. If we do not acknowledge God as the author of life and morals, we ultimately have to create our own meaning for life and make up our own rules. It's *people* trying to control their own thoughts and emotions, and then ultimately other people, based on what they think is right... which is based on either nothing or someone's feelings.

John Cleese said, "If people can't control their own emotions, then they have to start trying to control other people's behaviors."[1] This happens everywhere, including the church. So, if people make the rules, then *which* people decide what the rules should be? In society there is a saying, "Might makes right." If we all want to start dictating our own rules, then that saying is the logical conclusion.

The might says, "Do what I say."

The un-mighty says, "No."

Then the mighty subjugate the unmighty using force through money, "laws", weapons...

So who's ultimately "right"?

I believe Cleese was responding to people today who are offended by everything. We used to say, "free speech", but now the offendees of today say, "Hate speech." They don't see the laughable irony in what they are saying- they are *hating* the free speakers. But it's okay because they carry and display plenty of signs that say, "Love all," or "Peace and tolerance." OR perhaps the dumbest, most feckless statement of all: "Love is love." Can you imagine how short our dictionaries would be if we defined a word by the same word?! What is science? Well, science of course... and an animal is an animal, a car is a car... We hear this "love is love" moronic gibberish liberally spouted as if it meant something! What definition of love are they using? None!

When people then accept twaddling definitions like "love is love," then any bastardizing of words becomes acceptable. If we call something a hate crime based on what someone spoke, then there is no limit to the crime or criminal. This is a very dangerous trend as we let people such as the "hate speech" haters dictate what is right versus what God actually says is right. People will continue to chase their own thoughts and opinions down rabbit holes until it becomes completely backwards (2 Timothy 3-1-7).

For example, it could get to the ridiculous point that if I said I hate mosquitoes and would like to kill them all, the animal lovers would squeal, "All of life is precious *and equal*!" If you think I'm joking, Ingrid Newkirk the president of People for the Ethical Treatment of Animals

(PETA) said: "Animal liberationists do not separate out the human animal, so there is no rational basis for saying that a human being has special rights. They are all mammals."[2] But why stop at mammals? What about frogs, cute little turtles, and grasshoppers? If we accept this premise that all of life is equal, then if I squashed a mosquito, my previous genocidal mosquito comment may indict me of a hate crime. This seems absurd, however it is the direction our society is going as we get further and further away from God and His parameters on life.

"All of life is precious," say the animal lovers... unless, of course, it's a baby in the womb that you don't want... *God* says when life begins; *"For you formed my inward parts; you knitted me together in my mother's womb. I praise you, for I am fearfully and wonderfully made. Wonderful are your works; my soul knows it very well,"* (Psalm 139:13-14). The truth is rapidly becoming obsolete. When we see the videos of people desperately scrambling to save a whale that beached itself but ignore the tortured silent screams of children from the womb, we have lost all logical sanity and are living in a deep ungodly haze.

In fact, the Bible addresses calling something truth when it is not:

- *"Woe to those who call evil good and good evil who put darkness for light and light for darkness, who put bitter for sweet and sweet for bitter!"* (Isaiah 5:20).

- *"But understand this, that in the last days there will come times of difficulty. For people will be lovers of self, lovers of money, proud, arrogant, abusive, disobedient to their parents, ungrateful, unholy, heartless, unappeasable, slanderous, without self-control, brutal, not loving good, treacherous, reckless, swollen with conceit, lovers of pleasure rather than lovers of*

God, having the appearance of godliness, but denying its power. Avoid such people," (2 Timothy 3:1-5).

- *"For the time is coming when people will not endure sound teaching, but having itching ears they will accumulate for themselves teachers to suit their own passions,"* (2 Timothy 4:3).

- *"For we do not wrestle against flesh and blood, but against the rulers, against the authorities, against the cosmic powers over this present darkness, against the spiritual forces of evil in the heavenly places,"* (Ephesians 6:12).

- *"Let love be genuine. Abhor what is evil; hold fast to what is good,"* (Romans 12:9).

Without foundational, absolute truth, created by a God who loves us, then anything goes- anything can become right or wrong based on someone's opinion. The more that people try to set the boundaries for life, the more confusion, delusion, and hurt we will see. A huge example of this in our society today is "social media."

Social media is important to be in better communication with people we love, but we have lost the human touch. Hearing someone's voice is much more personal than seeing their writing. The more out of touch society gets with each other, the easier it is to push an agenda where there is no objective truth. There are so many pitfalls of social media that I could go on forever. I would say a vast amount of people's social interactions are lies. Who puts unflattering pictures of themselves on the internet? There was a news story of parents who ran a Healthy Living blog. Their polished blog image covered for the fact that they were living out of a car in a Walmart parking lot with five MALNOURISHED children in the car. They were arrested for child neglect.[3] This is just one example of exchanging truth for a lie. We are more concerned with our image on social media than about what is virtuous and true, to the point that we neglect our children because we would rather *appear* successful and happy.

Social media's instantaneous nature also has fueled a disturbing reactionary trend to just react rather than think and ask proper questions to discern the truth. This kind of overreaction without thought is extremely dangerous because it disregards another basic human right of "innocent until proven guilty." There are plenty of examples of this dangerous "tried by the instant social media" trend. This is especially wrong when Christians do this. They are reacting in hate- impatient and unkind. God gives a basic, biblical principle; *"Know this, my beloved brothers: let every person be quick to hear, slow to speak, slow to anger; for the anger of man does not produce the righteousness of God,"* (James 1:19-20).

The "rape" case of the Duke University men's lacrosse team in 2006 was a wakeup call to the dangers of hyper-reactionism and social media; and more recently, a similar rape accusation from Rolling Stone magazine where Phi Kappa Psi fraternity at University of Virginia was falsely indicted by this "pitchfork and fire" social media *before* there was suitable or corroborating evidence. These groups of men were heinously vilified with calls for castration and life imprisonment. There was no proof in either of these cases, yet because of instant media convictions, people shrieked and screamed and cried and spat on the innocents. The University of Virginia shut down the fraternity. The kids who lived through this maniacal circus were greatly harmed and some are still suffering from the consequences. Another huge problem with this instant, wrongful indictment by social media is that real people who are *actually* raped are not believed as easily. Again, if we do not follow what God says is true and good, we make up our own standards… This can lead to things like hysterical reactions without information, which ends up actually *hurting* others in an attempt to call for justice. God says, *"The way of a fool is right in his own eyes, but a wise man listens to advice,"* and; *"Do you see a man who is hasty in his words? There is more hope for a fool than for him,"* (Proverbs 12:15, Proverbs 29:20).

I also remember reading a gut-wrenching story of a mother and her young daughter. Her daughter was out "partying" and took several selfies that she sent to her mom. The mother asked how her daughter was doing, and she said something like, "I'm fine, mom." Her mom commented on how beautiful she looked and she seemed so happy. Shortly after, the daughter killed herself. I grieve and feel sick even typing this, because it is so far from what God wants for us. God's desire for us is to live full lives, in healthy relationships with real people, with real conversations. Satan's tactic is to make us feel isolated and alone. I believe social media does this. Though social media *appears* to help people connect more often, more quickly, in reality, it can isolate us and make us feel more alone, having less true friendships and more "Facebook friends" or "Instagram followers." We compare our lives to everyone else's seemingly "perfect" lives. Social media is NOT a replacement for what God says is good for us... community; relationship with Him and others. God says, *"How good and pleasant it is when God's people live together in unity!"* (Psalm 133:1) and *"Then the Lord God said, "It is not good that the man should be alone; I will make him a helper fit for him,"* (Genesis 2:18). OR *"Live in harmony with one another. Do not be proud, but be willing to associate with people of low position. Do not be conceited,"* (Romans 12:16). And numerous others.

The more we run from God and the parameters He set in place for our protection, the more we have to find meaning elsewhere, like social media. But now can be the time to stop running.

Actor Shia LaBeouf in a Q & A with *Interview* magazine, sums up well the personal struggles in life. He may be a tad more eccentric and nutty than the rest of us, but you have to excuse that a bit because he's an actor, after all. It was a fairly extensive interview, but here are couple highlights from it (Warning!! Naughty word content!):

> I've been a runner my whole life, running from myself. Whether to movies or drinking and drugging or fucking calamity or whatever it is, I've always been running. I'm a dude who loves delusion. It's why I love being an actor—I never have to actually look at myself or be faced with my shit or take responsibility… (ends with) … I've been blessed with a shit life.[4]

Crassly said, but the point is dead on. You can't be the person that you are right now, without the "shit" that you've created or endured. Often people run from themselves because they don't know what truth is, and are too afraid to take a hard look at themselves. Much of who you are was formed in your early toddler years that most of us can't even remember. You are right where you are, doing exactly what you're doing right now in life, initially based on someone else's decisions, but now based squarely on your own. Good or bad, it's where you are, but this can be the day to change. We all need to change for the better, so stop running from a God who loves you and embrace He who created you and knows what's best for you.

Christians and non-Christians have very similar problems about God. You can have a person that praised God all throughout their lives, but when severe difficulties hit, they say something like, "My God would never allow this. Therefore, I reject my belief." They were willfully ignorant of the horrors in the world as long as their lives were going well. But when THEY had something tragic happen to them... there no longer is a God. As long as it didn't happen to them, they were fine with their little pet God. HYPOCRITES! Can I hear an "AMEN" from the atheist leader! But you're no better atheists. I've talked with many of you who ultimately express that they too are mad at God and that's why they don't believe in Him. Help me out here atheists. How can you be mad at something you say doesn't exist? In fact, how can you be mad at anything, since there is no law of right and wrong? HYPOCRITES. Non-Christians hate Christians judging them but that is *exactly* what non-Christians do to Christians! They judge Christians and then use that to judge God, claiming He doesn't exist. It's laughable irony.

Christians are screwed up and so are you, non-Christians. You see, we have a lot in common! God even talks about screwed up people in the Bible. And believe me, there are many! Even most of the main patriarchs and leaders in the Bible were bad... some really bad, but God didn't squash 'em, He used them for His good purposes *after* they repented. Moses who wrote much of the Old Testament and led God's people out of Egypt was a murderer, and Paul (originally Saul), who wrote much of the New Testament was the leader of a group who *murdered* Christians, (Exodus 2:11-12, Acts 8:1). If the Bible is just a fable written by people trying to confuse or control the masses, why would they create a narrative with such horrible people? It's not logical unless God was demonstrating the reality of life and how screwed up we all are, needing of His guidance.

So non-Christians, if you continue slamming Christians for believing in a flying, purple, people- creator, just realize- you believe you exist from nothingness. Your life ultimately formed from nothing! My challenge to you all is this: seek God. If you don't believe in Him, that's no problem, nobody does until they do! Say to Him that you don't believe He is real, but *if* He is, ask Him to please make it clear. Don't put Him to infantile tests like asking Him to turn the ocean into pudding for you to believe. If you ask something like that, He knows your search is not real. Jesus said, *"Don't put God to the test,"* (Luke 4:12). As I said above, God is not your circus whipping bear to do *your* whims.

Truly search. On your search for reasons *not to believe*, search for reasons *to* believe as well. Or are you afraid you might find Him and don't really want to? If you truly seek Him, you will find Him. It's His promise. He works in mysterious ways and He doesn't often answer right away. We expect God to be patient with us and it is only fair that we are patient with Him. When people were seeking Jesus while he was alive, he spoke in parables. His disciples didn't like it and asked Him why didn't he just talk to them straight? Jesus responded, *"So they WILL NOT understand."* Although it sounds counterintuitive, Jesus was making it clear that if they really wanted to figure life out, then they would seek the answers by asking questions, (Matthew 11:25, Matthew 13:10-17). If you really want to find God, pursue the truth as Jesus said.

You may want to seek this great God but think you're too far gone for Him to care or help. You're wrong! God loves you, and Jesus says in Matthew 12:31, *"Therefore I tell you, EVERY sin and blasphemy WILL BE FORGIVEN people, but the blasphemy against the Spirit will not be forgiven."* And remember this, Jesus endured all the same temptations on Earth that we do, but he never gave up and he never gave in. He was even starved nearly to death when he didn't eat for forty days and THEN the devil put on as much pressure as possible to force Jesus to sin, but Jesus calmly said, *"Man shall not live by bread alone, but by every word that comes from the mouth of God,"* (Matthew 4:4). God doesn't want you to sin, but He's willing to forgive you repeatedly as long as you genuinely repent and ask Him. No sin is too awful for God to forgive except blaspheming the Holy Spirit, (a topic for another book). But suffice it to say that the majority of the populace is not guilty of this sin.

Also, God's Word is not complicated. His New Testament can't be super difficult to understand since it's about 200 pages shorter than a Harry Potter book. I may be in the minority, but I had more difficulty following who's who in the Harry Potter series than I did reading the

New Testament! God sums up life perfectly at the very end of Ecclesiastes 12:13-14, *"The end of the matter; all has been heard. Fear God and keep his commandments, for this is the whole duty of man. For God will bring every deed to judgment, with every secret thing, whether good or evil."*

Here are God's foundational building blocks for an eternal blissful life; **they are simple** and you don't need to put your thinking cap on for them:

- *"...if you confess with your mouth that Jesus is Lord and believe in your heart that God raised him from the dead, you will be saved,"* (Romans 10:9).

- *Love,* (1 Corinthians 13:4-8).

God requires these two steps first. However, He wants you to continue to grow up into the person He knows you can be (Hebrews 5:13-14). And we should want to because we love Him... because He first loved us, (1 John 4:13-21). And when we accept Him, God offers lasting joy and peace, contentment, fullness of life, and an eternal relationship with Him, your Creator. It doesn't mean life will be easy, it means you will know His Peace to deal with life.

9

Scientists Suck Too

The most brilliant person in the world is woefully ignorant compared to the vast complexities of life, nature, the universe(s), and the yet unknown. They mainly conjecture on ideas and theories in the small areas they have studied. The less intelligent do this as well. Some backwoods yahoo saying, "I think…" is the same statement as the most brilliant mind saying the same thing. Both are trying to reason. However, obviously, if it came to whose logic I would trust and believe in a situation of life and death, and I had to choose between the brilliant and the yahoo, I would pick the yahoo. Clearly. The yahoo would sustain my life with his backwoods knowledge of edibles versus poisons, how to capture game, how to fish, build shelter and fire… how to survive and thrive! The brilliant scientist could theorize about food while starving and/or freezing to death. However, the scientist most likely would be able to more articulately explain the biological degrading of their bodies and the nutrients the soil would absorb as they slowly and painfully died. After the backwoodsman saved your desperate life with his *knowledge*, you may even honor him by elevating his status to knighthood, or even call him, sir … Sir Yahoo.

I have one such "Sir Yahoo" customer who has a morel mushroom tattooed on his arm. I asked him about it, but it was hard to understand him. He had difficulty stringing a coherent sentence together through his yokel twang. He was what the world would call "truly dumb." But was he? He is the type of guy I was talking about in the intro. If the world came to survival, his knowledge would trump all else. And it IS knowledge. He didn't learn it by reading books, but he DID *learn* all his skills. So is he dumb? Clearly, no. In this case I would say the truly dumb one would be anyone who may arrogantly overlook and mock a beautiful person like this. When this guy left my store I said to the remaining people, "If the poop hit the fan, that guy would be eating lobster, covered with herbed morel mushrooms, and I would die by eating a gyromitra esulenta," (the poisonous mushroom that looks like a morel).

I love science, but not the arrogant, egotistical, superior-than-thou scientists. They are just as bad as the holier-than-thou Christians, but they get a pass because they are not, after-all, Christians. The scientific community's contemptuous ridicule of Christians is an odious double standard, and bitterly laughable. Scientists stack theory upon theory upon theory upon theory upon theory, and yet have the audacity to apprise the world through their upturned noses that their multi-layered theory was actually *factual*. It's like a theory Ponzi scheme where us simpletons bobble our heads up and down because we are not as intelligent as these wizards-of-smart. "Theory Ponzi"... you know... where the first "theory investment" is bogus but you keep stacking new theories, one on top of the other, all while citing the previous theory as one of the building blocks of proof for the whole "house of theories".

How old is the Earth? Scientists and their bobble-headed sycophants love to deride and lampoon some Christians who say the world is about 7,000 years old. They chortle as they peer over their round spectacles, "Doooo go on my good fellow," they say in their Thurston Howell III condescending voice. "Do enlighten us," (they pompously snicker). Scientists promulgate to us that the Earth is 4.543 billion years old. The bobbleheads bobble in "good little uneducated boy" agreement. Yet both are THEORIES. The 4.543 billion years is not a PROVEN fact!

It is a theory upon a theory upon a theory… The 7,000 year old earth is a THEORY as well. Both sides are arrogant in tenaciously believing themselves, but it's my observation that scientists are arrogant, with a cherry on top. There are numerous books that are written by both sides to try to support their own theory's side, but it doesn't mean they are factual. Not all theories are equal and many are false. It would behoove both sides to non-judgmentally listen, even if one is confident the other theory is wrong.

I wish science could factually disprove the God of Jesus because my life would be "easier." If God doesn't make the rules, then I do. If there is no official rule book, then I'm certainly not going to play by another human's rules. I'm playing by my own! However since I have come to believe Christianity is true, I realize the truth of Proverbs 26:12 that says, "Do you see a man who is wise in his own eyes? There is more hope for a fool than for him." But since I believe in God's Word I look to it and see what He says about the age of the earth. So what does He say? …Nothing. …He does not give an age. If God is not inclined to give the age of the earth, then neither am I. The Christians get 7,000 by looking at the genealogy listed in the Bible from when God created the world, and although I understand their theory, I don't accept their conclusion as a *fact*. Here is why: Did the earth exist before the formation of it? Yes. I know this will drive some Christians crazy, but all one has to do is look at the first two sentences of the Bible, "In the beginning, God created the heavens and the Earth. The Earth was without form and void, and darkness was over the face of the deep. And the Spirit of God was hovering over the face of the waters." What Earth? What deep? What waters? God hadn't even STARTED to create until verse three, which was day one. So it is crystal clear there was a heaven, a *formless* earth, the deep of space, and water. How long was all that stuff around? … Exactly… We don't know!

145

Conversely, science theorizes the age by expansion of the universe. But from what exactly? ... That's right, they don't know ... because it's a theory from a long time ago. And since the weatherman can't accurately predict tomorrow's weather, I'll place bets that scientists don't know the age of the Earth. However, I greatly appreciate the effort of scientists to try to come up with an educated guess.

As stated, I like Christ, but not so much Christians. I feel the same about scientists. A leading evolutionary biologist, who must have graduated high in his class of hoity-toityness, is Richard Dawkins. Anytime he debates or gets near to a Christian scholar, his face snidely scrunches up like a shar-pei dog. He sounds like a character that Monty Python would satirize. To be fair, Dawkins is a scientist, author, debater and reportedly intelligent. In a letter to his ten- year- old daughter he beautifully wrote about feelings and "love" but through a smudged scientific lens:

> People sometimes say that you must believe in feelings deep inside, otherwise you'd never be confident of things like "My wife loves me." But this is a bad argument. There can be plenty of evidence that somebody loves you. All through the day when you are with somebody who loves you, you see and hear lots of little tidbits of evidence, and they all add up. It isn't purely inside feeling, like the feeling that priests call revelation. There are outside things to back up the inside feeling: looks in the eye, tender notes in the voice, little favors and kindnesses; this is all real evidence.[1]

Ironically this sounds like more evidence of God who created love and feelings, than Dawkins' science. As he famously said in his book, *River Out of Eden*, "The universe that we observe has precisely the properties we should expect if there is, at bottom, no design, no purpose, no evil and no good, nothing but blind, pitiless indifference;" and another quote from the same book says, "DNA neither cares nor knows. DNA just is. And we dance to its music."[2]

So if Dawkins truly believes this, then he should think of his daughter with "blind pitiless indifference," and someone who can be neither good nor evil because she is just a product dancing to DNA's music. It SOUNDS ridiculous, because IT IS ridiculous and yet it is espoused by one who is supposed to be an elite thinker of our time… without even a whiff of irony! God sees Dawkins' daughter in a much different light. He knew and loved her before she was born, (Jeremiah 1:5). He knows every hair on her head, (Luke 12:7).

I've listened to many of Dawkins' lectures and debates. Listening to him is a bit like chewing on a cracker with no water… in the middle of the Sahara Desert. One of the debates I listened to was between Dawkins and John Lennox; you know… pop-n-fresh, the tiger killer from chapter two. But Lennox was more like a janitor in this debate… he mopped the floor with Dawkins. You can find John Lennox's debates online so I don't need to go any further. I have nothing against Dawkins personally and I appreciate his intelligence and his efforts in his scientific field, but I think his conclusions are about God and the truth of life is far off the mark.

Even though I poke fun at scientists, I appreciate their contributions of thought to the fields in which they were educated. Humility is a must though, which in my observation is in short supply. Again I say, they are woefully unenlightened in the magnitude of all that God created. Hey scientists, when have you, or anyone you've observed, created something new, something that's never existed, from absolutely nothing? Never! Man can create nothing original. Man can only "create" from the building blocks God has already created. I had a similar discussion with a customer and here is how it went:

A large, studly man entered my store for the first time. It was clear after a brief discussion this man was **Mensa** bright. I love people like this. It's a large part of how I learn. I've heard it asked numerous times from my friends and family, "How do you know 'that'?" If I was smart, I'd probably remember, but I just shrug my shoulders and say "I dunno…" I consider it a privilege to talk with these unrecognized geniuses. I ask many questions, sit back and soak in the rays of their minds. It's like vitamin D for the brain! But as well as listening, I relish the tête-à-tête. These are the people that help me fine tune my faith and learn to defend it better.

Shortly after he came in, I told him our "politics and religion" maxim. His response was one of my favorites, but I'll give the naughty word warning here again. He said, "So you talk about religion?" I said "Yep." After eyeing me up, assessing my level of seriousness and accepting that I was indeed serious, he said something very close to, "I believe Christianity is bullshit and anyone who believes in it is an idiot." Snowflake Christians would have melted under this affront. I busted out laughing. "Ahh refreshingly honest, straight to the point and… let the conversation commence!" I thought.

In intelligence, I was outmatched by Derek. I must say at the outset that even though Derek's words SEEMED harsh, he is one of the nicest people I have met. He is thoughtful and kind and I consider him a friend. Also, when I started to seriously consider writing this book, I asked Derek if he remembered that conversation so I could be as accurate as possible and he said yes but he didn't remember his words being quite that "harsh." Anyway, after he stated that Christians were idiots, I said, "You'll have to consider me an idiot then." He blanched and said something like, "Oh come on, you don't really believe that do you? It's a myth…" I said, "Yep, I believe it with all my heart and mind," and out of his kind heart he began to backtrack. I asked him NOT to relinquish the front he had created since he really believed what he said and told him I took no offense.

I had a strong feeling this was going to be a superb conversation mainly because Derek exhibited Godly "ethics." As stated, he was smart, but not to a point of arrogance. He was aggressive in speech, but not to a point of insisting on his own way. He was patient in listening and kind in speaking. He was not arrogant or rude and it was an honor to "lock horns" with him. I said kiddingly, "Since you think I'm an idiot, and you are clearly smart, it should be easy to defeat me in an argument, right?" He said, "I would think so." I said, "Wanna try?" to which he agreed. I asked if I could attempt to explain his understanding of the origins of life and his existence. He was game. I asked if he thought life could be explained scientifically and he said yes. So in an ultra-simplified way I said, "You believe in science, therefore, big bang, primordial soup, Darwinian evolution, mom+dad = Derek standing in front of me." He indulged me and said, "Basically, yes." I said, "Then I admire you because your faith is much greater than mine." A quizzical look skipped across his face as he said he didn't have faith. Since science is what he believes or trusts, it is therefore that in which he has faith, which is why I used the word. We agreed to call it "belief." So I said "Your *belief* is greater than mine." "How so?" Derek replied. "Because in order for you to exist, you have to believe in trillions upon trillions, (and I am GROSSLY *understating* the trillions,) of things that had to happen perfectly, sometimes simultaneously, and in exactly the perfect sequential order. Also your very first explanation of the origin of life and matter isn't even scientific."

Even though scientists' mental contortions try to explain the origins of life, there is never, nor will there ever be, a SCIENTIFIC explanation of something exploding from nothing. It belies the very definition of science and is therefore oxymoronic. Google defines it thusly: "science: the intellectual and practical activity encompassing the systematic study of the structure and behavior of the physical and natural world through observation and experiment." You CANNOT study the structure and behavior of the physical and natural world through observation and experiment of SOMETHING THAT DOES NOT EXIST, IN A NATURAL WORLD THAT IS NOT THERE, WITH OBSERVERS WHO ALSO DO NOT EXIST! It would be fine to say they don't have any idea where the "bangable" stuff came from, but don't insult people by saying scientifically something came from nothing. It's like saying the "Good Earth Fairy" made it.

Uh oh, I can hear the seething scientist now saying, "But that's what Christians believe, only they call the 'Good Earth Fairy,' God." To which I would agree. Where did God come from? Obviously no one knows. Christians like to say that He is the Alpha and Omega, the Beginning and the End. But is this any better than saying something came from nothing? Couldn't scientists say that stuff has "always been" just like Christians say God has always been? I would argue that yes, it would be an equally fair comparison. But both sides rant and rave about why they are right, yet neither can adequately explain. I think this puts creationists and scientists on equal footing about the origin of life and requires us to then explain and defend our theories starting from an "equal" argumentative base. This doesn't mean that the theories are equally valid. I believe it is far more difficult to defend the origin of the world from a scientific standpoint. And please do not bash me on this paragraph. The topic has been argued in thousands upon thousands of books for millennia. I understand I will not solve the matter with a facile paragraph in a book written by a pleb. I just ask the reader to understand the gist of the point.

Derek and I agreed that since I don't know where my God came from and he doesn't know where his stuff came from, we would argue from our knowledge of stuff and onwards. After admiring him for his "trillions upon trillions faith," I said, "My explanation of how I came to exist is simple. A loving God created me. I don't know why and I don't know how, but I thank Him. Every breath I take of His nutrient and element rich air, I thank Him for the wonder of the trillions of actions the body has to go through just to take the next breath. It's a marvel, or miracle if you like. It's implausible to believe it randomly happened by unimaginable mathematical luck, as scientists say. Scientists would have us believe that one could win the billion- dollar lottery trillions of times in a row for their world to exist. I like the joke, "Show me someone who plays the lottery and I'll show you someone who is bad at math."

Derek and I went at it for quite a while and at the end of our discussion, he gave me one of the greatest compliments I have ever received. He said something akin to, "Of all the books and years of study, you are the first one to get me to reexamine the idea of a real God." Derek would only come in a few times a year, but has sadly moved away. He will occasionally pop in when he comes to visit his relatives and I enjoy it every time.

As discussed with Derek, his belief or faith HAS to be greater than mine. The more I studied science, the more impressed I was with the sheer volume of what one must believe to have faith that science can explain life and everything that supports it. A website listed about two hundred major scientific disciplines, but each of those disciplines has numerous subdivisions, with many having hundreds of subdivisions. Some disciplines like those that study genes are so deep and specific that a scientist, or team of scientists, can study a single gene for their entire lives and perhaps at the end not know it's full function. In preparation for writing this book, I was studying the various disciplines of science. Fortunately for me, I quickly stopped when I came across an Epigeneticist. I listened to a two hour lecture on epigenetics. It was over my head, but it gave me a profound appreciation for how intricate and precise everything is interwoven and interdependent. God even says this in the Bible; *"For his invisible attributes, namely, his eternal power and divine nature, have been clearly perceived, ever since the creation of the world, in the things that have been made."* (Romans 1:20) and *"...Wonderful are your works; my soul knows it very well",* (Psalm 139:14). I believe people reading this right now know in their heart that a loving God created them, but don't want to admit it. M.D. Nabeel Qureshi, said, "As a student of medicine, one of the things that absolutely blew my mind, one of the things we took for granted quite regularly, was just how finely hinged life is on the precipice of death." As a result of his studies of both medicine, the body, and the Bible, Nabeel who was a professing Muslim converted to Christianity because the evidence was overwhelming.

If the trillions of bodily functions are not operating PERFECTLY, you get sick or die. We ignorantly take this for granted every day ironically BECAUSE they function so well! When our bodies go "bad," we blame God. Oddly, even people who don't believe in God blame God. Yet we rarely, if ever, thank Him for every breath we take... unless you're a severe asthma sufferer who knows how precious a single breath can be. Trillions of functions happening simultaneously may even be an under-exaggeration. But we'll stick with that number for analogy sake. How much is a trillion? If a person blinked continuously 1 trillion times in a row, how long would it take? If I did my math right, here are the numbers:

- 1 minute = 60 seconds
- 1 hour = 3600 seconds
- 24 hours = 86,400 seconds
- 365 days = 31,536,000 seconds
- Blinking takes about 1/10 of a second = 315,360,000 continuous blinks per year
- 1 trillion divided by the 315,360,000 blinks per year = 3170 years

152

It would take 3,170 YEARS to blink a trillion times in a row!

So "trillion" is a staggering number, but this is what your body does continuously every day. Probably every nanosecond, but I'm not greedy.

Also impressive is the precision of automobiles, how finely tuned they are in order for them to function properly, but they are like a kid's sandbox toy compared to the God-made human body! How fantastic is the atheist's belief that these things happened randomly and by chance from absolutely nothing! Such faith should be admired! ...ooor pitied.

The body is infinitely complicated, but the vast world and all that's in it dwarfs the miracle of the body. So as UNBELIEVABLE as it is to believe the body randomly came to be, it is far more fantastic to believe the universe and all the elements needed for basic life POPPED into existence from zero... nothing at all. That's right, kids, science would have us believe that a myriad amount of stuff as big as suns and planets exploded into existence from... nothing. BUT WAIT, the planet Earth in order to sustain life, had to explode just so perfectly, it needed to be a precise distance from the sun, a meticulous axis tilt, a punctilious spin, plus all the scrupulously placed chemicals and elements for any chance that life could survive. Any deviation, and life would not happen. Hugh Ross who has a doctorate in astrophysics, kindly puts this chance of life at 1 in 10 to the 282 power, which is 10 with 282 zeros after it. For the mathematically challenged or the more visual reader, the serendipitous improbability of life may be:

.000000000000000000000000000000000000000000000000000
000000000000000000000000000000000000000000000000000000
000000000000000000000000000000000000000000000000000000
000000000000000000000000000000000000000000000000000000
000000000000000000000000000000000000000000000000000001.

As I suggested in the discussion with Derek, I believe the chance is zero. But Hugh Ross and I are actually pretty close to each other; I say zero because nothing comes from nothing, and he says practically zero. An infinite, almighty God said He did it, which is far more plausible. I think one of the worst aspects of the BIG BOOMERAMMA is that it's taught as FACT. The scientific explanations of life such as the "big bang" perhaps may be true, but they leave out the critical aspect that God "banged" it. Scientists are attempting to explain creation with the laws of science that God created, yet without giving credit where it is due! I have no problem in people trying to explain why things exist, but when they leave God out of the explanation, you really have to go to your imagination station in LaLa-ville to pull a magic universe out of your hat. (I was going to say ass, but hat will do. I don't want to offend anyone after all.)

People need to scrutinize science and scientists like they do God. It's funny, often when we observe the difficulties of life, many conclude that there is no God. Yet when scientists pass off hooey theories that are eventually discredited we don't conclude that there is no science or scientists. We just rightly decide to go back to the drawing board and search for new theories that attempt to explain the data more accurately. If we give this gracious latitude to scientists, how much more should we extend it to God? So scientists are given the benefit of the doubt, but the creator of science- NAH. The data is in on God we're told and he doesn't exist, so... end of discussion.

In rehashing this theory-upon-theory Ponzi scheme, it's important to point out the inherent nature of confirmation bias. For those who don't know what this is, it's defined as "the tendency to interpret new evidence as confirmation of one's existing beliefs or theories." Confirmation bias is often used against Christians who may use tautological explanations like, "I believe in God because I have faith." And when asked why they have faith they would say, "because I believe in God." So they are simplistically confirming what they already believe. Theory-upon-theory is the same. They are using unproven ideas to "prove" what they believe. As an example, since most scientists don't believe in God, they don't consider Him as a possibility to the answer. They are confirming their bias that the only logical explanation is often an illogical scientific explanation. They pile poop upon poop in the hope it doesn't fall over and make a mess.

Why do people accept these theories as fact? Because they are *taught* as fact. Therefore, people believe the theories to be true and no longer question them. When no one questions, you win the debate by default. Students are taught at an early age that man evolved from the ape. There is scarcely any real physical connection between the two, but the theory is still shoveled into students' brains. Scientists use scant "evidence" of the "missing link" such as Lucy the apewoman, but are students informed that the evidence is just a few fragments of a skull that has been artistically pieced together? Hell no, that would expose their weak evidentiary narrative. Do a search on "Lucy the missing link" and see how much of the skull remains and then look at the artist's imaginative recreation of Lucy. It's laughable, but taught as a real ape to human link. This lie was foisted on the public until it was brought to light, and *then* they admitted they used more imagination than fact in recreating what Lucy looked like. But if it hadn't been challenged, science would have been perfectly content with perpetuating this lie because they are trying to confirm their bias that humans came from apes. Lucy is not the only attempt at forcing a lie. For fun just review Piltdown man, Nebraska man, Java man or Orce man.

If an artist is *creating* the "missing link" then let's call it art and not science. I am an artist and have great respect for art and most artists. But let's give art credit where it is due. God is the true artist because He designed it all from the start and artists are trying to guess at the look of what He designed from the leftover bones. I like the creative way artists

155

render unknown species based on skeletons found, but, again, let's not pass the artist's interpretation as factual evidence. As an example, what do we know about dinosaurs? We know they existed because we have unearthed their bones. What don't we know? We don't know their age, why, or how they died out. We don't know their color or ultimate shape. As an illustration of this, if we didn't know what an elephant looked like and we found it's bones, an artist would have to draw it without a trunk or ears since there are no bones in either. So the illustrations and recreations are mere postulations.

As much as scientists say there is plenty of evidence for Darwinian *evolution*, it is mostly theory. But let's take a brief look at Darwinian evolution. We factually know there are apes and humans, but ALL the missing "in between" pieces to this THEORY are, as stated, artistically added… and regretfully passed onto the bobbleheads as fact. If Darwinian ape-changing-to-human were a fact, there would be plenty of linking evidence. There isn't. You would think that over the millions of years that apes were supposedly evolving into humans, they would have found myriads of examples. There would be no need to manipulate data to fool people. The link would be obvious. If scientists were truthful, they would say there are virtually no linking fossil facts to show one species changing to another; in fact there are distinguished arguments against this. If species have been changing into altogether different species for millions of years, there would be an overwhelming fossil record of this… nope, doesn't exist. If species were intersexed this way, a cat should theoretically be able to mate with a dog or a horse with a pig… nope, doesn't work that way. If ape evolved into man why can't man get an ape pregnant? Or vice versa? Why isn't the world populated with these man/ape breeds now? Why would they be distinctly separate now? Sure scientists would have some kind of explanation, but they are extrapolating from very little evidence. It would be fair to listen to an alternative opinion, but that is rarely allowed in schools. It almost seems like science is trying to dupe the willfully ignorant by saying, "Well look how close the ape resembles us. Therefore we must have evolved from them." People can more easily buy this explanation because they can *see* how much more similar we look to the ape than, say, the giraffe.

Scientists then point to how similar our DNA is to the ape. This is another *theory*. Our makeup IS very similar to apes… and fruit flies. It's been suggested recently that we are more similar to pigs than apes, but that would be a tougher sell since humans don't look very piggy. We are also decidedly similar to… dirt! That's right, the majority of elements in the human body are the same in dirt; carbon, hydrogen, nitrogen, calcium, phosphorous, potassium, sulfur, sodium, chlorine, magnesium, silicon… Scientists may say this shows we came from the same origin, but I would argue that it shows God used the same elemental building blocks for all life. And what is it that God said? *"From dust we were created and to dust we will return."* Here Genesis 3:19 reminds us precisely what happens when we die. Our bodies' elements break down and nourish the soil! Sounds like God knew what He was talking about.

Also plaguing the scientific community is the current state of politics and agendas. Today we can't talk about global warming because we are told the science is settled. Whether or not man-made global warming exists, saying science is "settled" is unprofessional and honestly, unscientific. The beauty of science is that we CONTINUE to learn, supporting or adjusting what is known to create a more accurate picture of truth. Science should never be "settled"! As soon as anyone makes a statement like this, it is prudent to see who and how the study is being funded. Much of science today is financed by individual companies or government agencies with specific agendas. For the science money to keep flowing, the scientists naturally will try to keep the donor appeased. And yes, the government has agendas too. This doesn't necessarily mean that the science is bogus but it does mean we need to consider it as a factor that the information may be skewed.

You don't have to look too far to see how scientists have been pressured to tell outright lies or gross fabrications based on agendas. To be fair, I don't know if the scientists are fully aware of the outlying agenda. But there are times when scientists' personal bias is evident. I've heard many scientists ask, "Where is the proof of your God?" But as I've shown above, science often operates on scant "proof," yet expects us to believe it. However I will endeavor to briefly answer this question, and add a few more details in the next chapter. So if the scientist says, "Where is your God?" I would answer, "Where is your mom?" Think about it. If a four-year-old child was constantly, tenaciously, clinging to his mom, we would say that was unhealthy. If a twenty-one-year-old was clinging to his mom, we would say that's weird and there's a problem. So why would we expect God to be there constantly for us whenever we ask? It would be just as weird. God wants us to grow up and participate in the process of living and learning about life by overcoming the challenges so we can live a more intellectually healthy and abundant life.

As for evidence of God, there is PLENTY to conclude that a masterful Creator is behind all this stuff that sustains us perfectly. Though God is not seen, everything He made is clear. If I stumbled across a gorgeous, fully furnished house in the middle of the woods; I would assume that someone built it, whether I saw the person build it or not. It's just that simple. Just because something can be explained scientifically doesn't mean God didn't create it. It is far more logical to think that God created our brains and senses in order to discern that He created nature and the scientific principles we use to observe and study.

There are many biblical stories that scientists try to discredit such as Noah and the ark. They say there is no chance Noah and a few others could have built such a massive wooden ship. They say that even the best shipbuilders in the world today with all the modern tools couldn' build it. So is that it? Science says it's not possible, so it's not? No other explanation will do? Well, similar to what I explained with the creation of the world, I look to see what God's Word actually says. The story itself is only *three pages* long- 2,144 words. Moby Dick is three hundred seventy-eight pages or 206,052 words! One story talked about the ultimate corruption of people, building a massive vessel, gathering animals, flooding the world that ends in a cataclysmic way for all its inhabitants, and finally culminating into the beginning of new life. And the other talked about a white whale. So how much could we possibly know about the Noah story in THREE pages?- obviously, very little.

Could tens of thousands of people have helped Noah? I can just hear the helpers now; "Suuuure Noah, we'll help you build your gigantic boat... you crazy old bat." Did God help Noah? The Bible doesn't say except that God told him his mission, and sealed him in the ark. It is fair to believe that God helped him in numerous other ways, but only included the most pertinent information in the story. But it is faulty and unfair thinking to say that something DIDN'T happen because it isn't explicitly stated in the Bible. If the Bible was comprehensive in every detail, it would be so many volumes, nobody would bother reading it. In fact, at the end of the book of John, (21:25), it says, *"Now there are also many other things that Jesus did. Were every one of them to be written, I suppose that the world itself could not contain the books that would be written."* So not everything is recorded in the Bible, only what we *need* to know. But again, just because it doesn't say, doesn't mean it didn't happen.

Let's take a look at Stonehenge or the Egyptian pyramids. These structures were made of massive stones- some weighing as much as fifty tons. They were so precisely placed or interconnected that people wonder how it could have been completed with normal people and ancient tools. Some people suggest aliens must have done it because they don't have another "logical" explanation for how ancient humans could have accomplished that. What proof do we have of aliens doing it? None, but people seem to be more willing to believe in aliens building something with zero evidence, than Noah building an ark with written and archaeological corroboration. However, there possibly is a *biblical* answer for precisely building gargantuan structures back then. There was a race of people called the Nephilim who were apparently huge and very skilled. In Genesis 6:5 it says they were mighty men of renown. All the people were afraid of them because, as Caleb said, *"We are like grasshoppers compared to them,"* (Numbers 13:33). How many Nephilim were there?- thousands? millions? We don't know. Could they have built these vast ancient structures or perhaps helped Noah with the ark? The Nephilim are not mentioned often in the Bible, but ironically they are mentioned directly before the story of Noah. Interestingly, it says the Nephilim were on the earth during Noah's time AND afterward, which means Noah would either have to be one of these huge guys or carried the genes of the Nephilim since everyone died in the flood except for Noah and his family. It's biblically plausible since God's Word doesn't say yes or no.

Scientifically and biblically there is still a substantial amount that we don't know. The Bible tells about many civilizations and people that we have or had no physical evidence of. In the past, God skeptics said there was that proof of many of the big names in the Bible like Pontius Pilate or King David ever existed and used this to cast doubt on the authenticity of the Bible. However, years later archeologists unearthed artifacts that proved the existence of both. Archeology is proving to be a thorn in the side of God deniers. Almost everything dug up at "biblical" sites shines the light that God's Word was dead-on accurate. One of those major sites was the caves at the Dead Sea, found in 1947. There were hundreds of documents and tens of thousands of fragments uncovered, scientifically dated hundreds of years B.C. (Before Christ). The God haters were sure this amount of evidence would be the death-knell of the Bible and Christianity. They were convinced that they would uncover glaring inconsistencies and errors with the information they found and the Bible which was already written. What they found was the opposite. Most of the evidence corroborated what was already recorded in the Bible. The "proof" of God and His Word was significantly advanced. Unearthed "pages" of the Old Testament were dated before Christ was born and contained prophecies of Jesus and the life he would live. The OLD Testament prophecies are unmistakably talking about Jesus and written hundreds to thousands of years before he lived. Please do your own research and look at the chapter titled, God is Dead?, where many of the verses are cited. So science through archeology and dating methods was instrumental in showing prophecies of Jesus to be true. God's instruments of science undergird His instrument of instruction- His written Word.

Christians are required to study this written Word and are often mocked by scientists for not being able to answer all of life's questions. This is completely unfair for *people* to demand this. It would be similar to demanding that scientists have all the answers to all disciplines of science. Would it be fair to ask a chemical scientist about psychological science or oceanography or mathematics or epigenetics? If "no," then why is a Christian mocked for not knowing all the answers of God and life?! There is a caveat though- God DOES require Christians to have a ready answer to anyone who asks, (1 Peter 3:15). So Christians need to continuously study God's Word, life, history, and science to give a valid accounting of their belief. Christians should be the true intellectuals then. Scientists usually study a mere branch of science, but a Christian needs to study the WHOLE tree.

Scientists create theories. God creates scientists. Scientists have to reinvent the definition of "science" in order to explain the origin of life or Big Bang, i.e.- an unfathomable amount of stuff never comes from nothing. What if Christians defined God one way and then when trapped, say, "That was the former definition of God, but now God is this…" Would scientists accept this redefinition or would they rightly laugh?

161

Scientists and science are tremendously valuable to *all* aspects of life. But when scientist egoism supplants God, the truth often gets skewed. God is the Alpha and Omega, the Beginning and the End. He has been biblically defined for thousands of years and that definition has remained constant. So science isn't the constant, God is.

10

Nature Never Goes Out Of Style

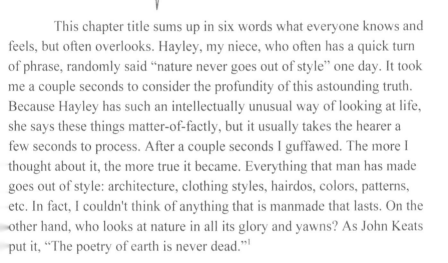

This chapter title sums up in six words what everyone knows and feels, but often overlooks. Hayley, my niece, who often has a quick turn of phrase, randomly said "nature never goes out of style" one day. It took me a couple seconds to consider the profundity of this astounding truth. Because Hayley has such an intellectually unusual way of looking at life, she says these things matter-of-factly, but it usually takes the hearer a few seconds to process. After a couple seconds I guffawed. The more I thought about it, the more true it became. Everything that man has made goes out of style: architecture, clothing styles, hairdos, colors, patterns, etc. In fact, I couldn't think of anything that is manmade that lasts. On the other hand, who looks at nature in all its glory and yawns? As John Keats put it, "The poetry of earth is never dead."[1]

Numerous other poets rightfully sing nature's praise:

- "I felt my lungs inflate with the onrush of scenery- air, mountains, trees, people. I thought, 'This is what it is to be happy.'" Sylvia Plath[2]

- "The earth has its music for those who will listen." Reginald Holmes[3]

- "Adopt the pace of nature. Her secret is patience."
  Ralph Waldo Emerson[4]

Or perhaps Abe Lincoln summed it up best: "I can see how it might be possible for a man to look down upon the earth and be an atheist, but I cannot conceive how he could look up into the heavens and say there is no God."[5]

One such poetic lady came into our store. She had a lyrical tempo to her carefully calculated words. I so appreciated the conversation that I had to include it here:

One day, a chic, middle-aged lady entered my shop. Like most people who come in, we started talking, and at some point I asked her what makes her tick, you know, what she likes, studies, and believes. She said something like, "I'm a cosmic universalist." I don't think I have this title exactly correct, but it is close. Not knowing what that was, I said I was excited to listen to her thoughts. She seemed doubtful I would want to hear her beliefs since I had already tipped my hand at my thoughts on life earlier in the conversation. I had to convince her I actually did want to hear what a cosmic universalist was because I had never met one and wasn't sure I would again. She had an unusually beautiful way of phrasing and expressing her words. If she read the 10 million- word, federal tax codes to me, I think I would have listened all the way through and given her a standing ovation at the end. A very loose summation of her belief was that we are all part of the natural cosmos through complex personal interactions, but ultimately it all comes down to love and how we embrace it. Wrapping up her explanation, she gave me a sideways glance probably thinking I was going to call her a kook. On the contrary, there was hardly anything she said I disagreed with and I praised her ability to communicate it so eloquently. Through her own personal search for truth, she basically found and described God and His creation.

Instead of pointing out that most of what she believed was straight out of the Bible, I simply asked who or what brought her ideas into existence. She dithered in her answer and then said, "I know you would want me to say God." She was wrong. I wasn't fishing for an answer so I could force the conversation toward God. I just thought she would have a unique perspective. She hesitated again as she engaged her very capable mind and came up with one word; she said, "Mystery." NOT, "It's a mystery," just "Mystery." To clarify, I asked if she purposefully chose just this one word, and she confirmed that it was purposeful. As was unique to her verbal style, she was using "mystery" more as an entity than a description. I smiled with joy at her using a word that God uses for Himself, for Jesus and His ways:

- *"That their hearts might be comforted, being knit together in love, and unto all riches of the full assurance of understanding, to the acknowledgement of the mystery of God, and of the Father, and of Christ, in whom are hid all the treasures of wisdom and knowledge,"* (Colossians 2:1-3).

- *"...how the mystery was made known to me by revelation, as I have written briefly. When you read this, you can perceive my insight into the mystery of Christ, which was not made known to the sons of men in other generations as it has now been revealed to his holy apostles and prophets by the spirit,"* (Ephesians 3:3-5).

- *"Now to him that is of power to establish you according to my gospel, and the preaching of Jesus Christ, according to the revelation of the mystery, which was kept secret since the world began,"* (Romans 16:25).

- *"...But in the days when the seventh angel is about to sound his trumpet, the mystery of God will be accomplished, just as he announced to his servants the prophets,"* (Revelation 10:7).

- *"Oh, the depth of the riches both of the wisdom and knowledge of God! How unsearchable are His judgments and unfathomable His ways! For who has known the mind of the Lord, or who has been his counselor?"* (Romans 11:33-36).

(If you want more verses on God's mystery, here are a few additional: Luke 8:10, Ephesians 3:9, 1 Corinthians 2:7, Colossians 1:26, Ephesians 1:9, Romans 16:25).

I mentioned to this woman that "Mystery" may actually be a title that would please God if she would recognize that the mystery *is* God. She responded by simply saying, "Oh." God says to seek Him and you will find Him. But you must really try to seek Him. Most people today seek to NOT find Him and when they don't find Him they say, "See, there is no God!" This is like if you play hide and seek with a friend and the seeker chooses not to seek but rather sit in one spot. Then you declare, "See! My friend cannot be found! He must not exist!" This lady found the essence of God by seeking for the truth. I told her that she was just a whisper away from completely knowing Him by just simply reaching out and acknowledging the Mystery who created all that she had beautifully explained.

The beauty of nature is that it engages every one of our physical senses. If you are blind, deaf, or crippled, you still love nature. In fact, people with these life conditions often have a greater appreciation of nature. You might think it would be unfortunate that a blind man cannot see nature's glory. But he may respond by asking if you *heard* the numerous distinct bird warbles, or the buzz of the bee, or *felt* the quick, cool wisp of air that just blew past your cheek, or *tasted* the essence of the flowers that wafted into the air as you walked through them. Sight is fantastic and a wonderful gift from the Creator, but when we take it for granted, our other senses become dull. This gives the blind man a heightened awareness of nature and, counterintuitively perhaps, an advantage. The grandeur of nature is limitless... fall leaves, mist, the sound of waves, a cool breeze, grass between your toes, mountains, prairies, waterfalls, flowers by the millions, echoes, the rumble of thunder, stars in the blackness of night, sunrise, sunset, the arctic, the warming sun, pine forests, deserts, the myriad of brilliant colors, smell of burning wood, rainbows, four seasons... it speaks to us- mind, body and soul.

The Creator of nature's glory said that Solomon, in all his splendor, was not comparable to something as simple as the lilies of the field. Go ahead and search online for "field lilies" and see a tiny fraction of God's spectacular creation. It's amazing just to see the pictures. But imagine yourself standing there, surrounded by these flowers, and how awe-inspiringly beautiful it would be! Come on man, no one can look at these gorgeous lily fields and say with a shoulder shrug, "Ehh..." God's creation is AWESOME.

Come on naturalists, you are looking at God's divine nature, and you know it in your heart. You want to be one with nature because He created you *from* nature (Genesis 2:7) so that you could share in it with the Artist of nature, (Romans 1:19-21, Ecclesiastes 3:11). This makes sense! Think about it. You feel connected to nature because the Creator created both you AND the natural world. You are so intricately a part of it that after you die, you turn back into nature to replenish the soil! Feeling a part of nature reminds me of a conversation that I had with my God-hating relatives:

Relatives of mine, a married couple, are hypersensitive to anything religious. I'll refer to them as Bob and Sue in this story. The slightest whiff of Christianity becomes instant indignation. They have lived out of state for most of my life and I have had very little interaction with them. But whenever I have hung out with them, I've enjoyed them. They are smart, earthy, and engaging, with a zest for living. I love them and always look forward to sharing in life when they are around. But there is one subject I have never broached with them over all these decades, and that is my faith. You see, they are preachers of tolerance unless it comes to Christians, of whom they are utterly intolerant and contemptuous. Unfortunately, I think their hypocrisy is lost to them. I have known of their great hatred of religion for decades. I felt to engage them in anything remotely Christian would be to ostracize our companionship and possibly make it so I would have zero interaction with them.

Relating with others is often difficult. We say stupid stuff that drives people away. Look no farther than all the relationship heartaches in the world. Without a balance in life and relating we will spiral out of control. The Byrds song, "Turn, Turn, Turn," reminds me of this harsh, and positive balance of life. The words are straight out of the Bible from Ecclesiastes 3:1-8:

> *There is a time for everything,*
> *and a season for every activity under the heavens:*
> *A time to be born and a time to die,*
> *a time to plant and a time to uproot,*
> *A time to kill and a time to heal,*
> *a time to tear down and a time to build,*
> *A time to weep and a time to laugh,*
> *a time to mourn and a time to dance,*

A time to scatter stones and a time to gather them,
a time to embrace and a time to refrain from embracing,
A time to search and a time to give up,
a time to keep and a time to throw away,
A time to tear and a time to mend,
a time to be silent and a time to speak,
A time to love and a time to hate,
a time for war and a time for peace.

Verse 7 says *"...a time to be silent and a time to speak..."* Since my relatives were acrimonious when talking about God then it does a disservice to force a conversation. God does not believe in forcing Himself on anyone and **if it's good enough for Him, it should be good enough for me.** His definition of love specifically states that it does not *insist* on its own way, (1 Corinthians 13:5). I have stated this before, but God loves them more than I possibly could. I felt the only thing I had to offer them was myself, prayers, and to love them as God asked me to. I have been praying for them for decades. I hoped a time would come to organically share the truth about God with them. It did.

My mother called me a couple years ago and asked if this couple could sleep over at my house. I was really surprised considering they had never even visited, let alone spent the night. My first thought was that one of them was dying. They were not dying, but I still don't know why exactly they came for this visit. I happily said that they could stay at my house because I like their company.

Early Sunday morning, I was sitting in the dining room, eating the spectacular breakfast I had just made, (if I do say so myself). I was sipping my coffee when they sat down and joined me. Usually, I go to church with my wife even though I don't like "church," but since my relatives were there, I decided to be a heathen, (as the church might call me,) and stay back to talk with them instead. We were chit-chatting when my wife, (who does like church), was headed out the door and said, "Well I'm headed to worship the Lord!" This was received with eye-rolling and mouth-corner-pinching from my relatives. This started the ball rolling with Sue making a mildly antagonistic, anti-Christian, generic comment, to which I laughed because I mostly agreed with her. Bob asked why I laughed and I told him I was in the process of writing a book about the subject of Christians' *un*love. They were intrigued and asked what the book was about. I warned them that they probably didn't want to know since it was a religious subject, but they persisted in asking so I told them the title. "God is Great, But His People Suck," I blurted. Their reaction was the same as everyone else: with laughter and the "ain't that the truth" response. They asked about the content and I once again gave them the choice to opt-out of the conversation since it was about the God in whom I believe. Sue then said something I now hear often. "I don't mind talking about God as long as it is like this." I was sure I knew what she meant but I asked her anyway. She said that as long as we were simply talking WITH each other, she didn't mind the subject. Once again, I agreed with her. It was a level talking field, not one where one side considers their point to be more worthy of being heard. Most people don't mind being talked WITH, but no one likes being talked AT. So off we went into a VERY religious discussion with wonderful sharing of personal stories. It was a joy.

The talk with my relatives was earthy and beautiful. At one point, Sue shared about an experience she had with nature where she said she *literally* felt like she was part of all of nature- everything- the trees, the ground, smell, touch... As I understood it, she seemed to be saying that she was no longer just human, but human and nature combined. Some people would think that was nuts, while others would nod their heads in accepting comprehension. I understood, and acknowledged her passionate honesty. From the outsider looking in, I'm sure she didn't physically change into the wind, or tree or dirt, but she personally *felt* like she did. God sometimes allows people to experience Him in different ways. Just because it didn't happen to you or isn't the way God would try to reach you, doesn't mean it doesn't happen for others. God created Sue, God created nature, and Sue experienced it ethereally. BUT, sadly, she didn't recognize or thank the Artist.

Although this couple enjoys the beauty of life, it has also jaded them against God. It has been a life of tragedies, pain, and sorrow enough for a dozen people. The female part of the duo has had to endure the lion's share of the pain. There are numerous ways to cope with life's unfairness, but I believe they initially chose blaming God... out of existence. In fact, I think this is logical to some degree. If God gave us this life and it turned out to be calamitous, then ipso facto, God is evil. If then God is evil but says He is love, He therefore cannot exist. Once you accept this premise, it becomes easy to live behind a filter of cynicism and to hate anyone espousing the contrary. However logical that might *seem*, it doesn't mean it is correct. We weren't born with a guaranteed good life sticker. Life is harsh for almost everyone. In fact, it is promised to be harsh at times by God for two main reasons: 1) disobedience and 2) to be tougher and build character.

- 1) If God did make us, and the rules of nature and life, then He has every right to set parameters. If we know the rules and the consequences of breaking those rules and then deliberately defy God by doing the opposite of what He set up, it is logical for God to punish and for us to suffer the consequences. It *IS* fair. God prepared a beautiful world and told its first inhabitants it was theirs to enjoy. He set up only *one* command, which was to not eat from just a *single* tree. At the time it would have been very easy to obey since there were plenty of other trees and fruit. But Eve and later Adam decided to test God's dictum of death with... uh... rather *unfruitful* consequences. The punishment was harsh and did ultimately result in death, but initially Adam was told that he would now have to work hard in order to eat. God put strife between husband and wife and kicked them out of this perfect garden of Eden. Just to make sure they knew He was serious about this banishment, angels with flaming swords were put in place to guard the garden entrance, (Genesis 3:15-24).

- 2) Now that the world was sinful and we needed to deal with this new evil and harshness, God knew we needed to be toughened up to. There is no way to do this without difficult work. Initially God provided and wanted Adam to work and keep the garden of Eden. (Genesis 2:15), but after Adam sinned God greatly increased the labor! (Genesis 3:16-19). However, God says He disciplines those that He loves, (Proverbs 3:12, Hebrews 12:6). This may initially sound backwards, but if you think about what your greatest achievements are, you'll recall that they are the result of difficult labor. No premier athlete is impressive without racking their body through painful training, and no prosperous business is built without scrimping, saving, and sleepless nights. Better marriages are built by going through difficult disagreements and working them out. There are numerous examples that prove hard work produces positive results. A coach often seems harsh when he pushes his protégé to try harder and reach for a higher goal. He does this not to be a jerk, but because he wants to see the athlete improve to be the best he can be. This is exactly why God now tests us and puts us through harsh trials. He wants us to try harder so that we can be better. He wants us to figure life out without being given or told everything. He wants us to be pure gold by putting us through fire just like gold has to be in order for it to be refined, (1 Peter 1:6-9).

At one point during our talk, Sue said she doesn't believe in any religion, but if she followed any belief it would be Buddhism. I could understand this because of what Buddha set out to do- find truth and love, (exactly what God asks us to do). However, I didn't share my thoughts about Buddhism during this particular conversation because I was more focused on listening to my relatives. I acknowledge the appreciation of Buddha *if* the words attributed to him were actually his. Like Buddha, Jesus' words are often challenged by skeptics stating we can't be sure that he actually spoke them. It is curious then, that these people, like Sue, willingly accept the words of Buddha, who we don't *factually* know existed. It is likely that Buddha was an actual person, but there are no historical or archaeological records of his lifetime to provide a date of birth or death. We know far less about Buddha than Jesus. Buddha is said to have lived 500 to 600 years before Jesus and Buddha's first words were finally written hundreds of years after the time he lived- words which were previously passed on through oral tradition. **Buddha's words are only *circumstantially* known. Some of you might think that the same applies to Je**sus since we do not have any known documents that he *wrote*, but we do have historical and archeological evidence of what he spoke, dated to within approximately thirty years of his death on a cross. Along the same line of thought- Julius Caesar is another historic figure whose history is never questioned, though little of his life is FACTUALLY recorded and much of what we think we know of him is from a fictitious play by Shakespeare, called *The Tragedy of Julius Caesar,* written around 1599.

Accepting the premise that Buddha existed and said some of the things attributed to him, he appeared to be a man on a very important quest. He was searching for the truth in life. I would say he was searching for love… and for the most part, found it. He was searching for the truth that was already placed in his heart by God. He found what God later revealed in 1 Corinthians 13:4-8:

Love is patient and kind; love does not envy or boast; it is not arrogant or rude. It does not insist on its own way; it is not irritable or resentful; it does not rejoice at wrongdoing, but rejoices with the truth. Love bears all things, believes all things, hopes all things, endures all things. Love never ends.

If you look at the writings attributed to Buddha, you will see much of them speak to these simple verses. According to legend, Buddha was dissatisfied for years with different teachings and struck out on his own to learn the truth and meaning of life. To which I say amen. Everyone should go on this personal search for why they exist. I respect people who take this journey even if they conclude other than what I have. I don't respect those who don't think at all of why they exist, (because they just wanna party, man), or believe something just because they grew up that way, or someone else told them what to think.

In fact, Roman, my adult son, said to me several years ago, "Dad I don't want to believe something just because you believe it." In this case he was speaking about my faith. I said, "Great! I wouldn't want you to believe it just because I believe it. I would want you to search for truth yourself and come to your own conclusion based on the best evidence." If you believe something just because someone else believes it, that's no belief at all! I asked him to not be lazy and plod through life, but to really seek the truth. He did end up writing down several pages of notes, comparing and contrasting religions, and ended up concluding that Christianity was true. This is precisely what God asks us to do. He doesn't say, "Yeah, thou shaltest believe unto me becauseth someone hath toldest thoust to." He says that if we seek Him we will find Him. Unfortunately, most people don't bother seeking the truth and often those who do "seek," seek to *not* find God by saying something like, "God, gimme a lot of stuff NOW; if you don't, I know you don't exist… uh… Amen."

I was so appreciative after the lengthy "nature" and religious discussion with Bob and Sue that I later called them that same day to thank them. Bob's response surprised me, "It was wonderful, we couldn't stop thinking and talking about it our whole way driving home." He also added that they would like to continue the discussion. "So would I," I said.

Sue experienced the ethereal beauty of nature, but there is the factual, scientific aspect of nature as well. The study of nature's provisions solves difficult problems. To be sure, science and nature are inextricably linked, but to some degree I think scientists have blinded themselves and are "solving" problems by potentially creating worse ones. Genetically mutating food, the global warming agenda and natural healing are a few of the areas that would be wise to examine.

I used to believe science had most of the answers to healing the body. Wow, was I ignorant! Now I believe almost one hundred and eighty degrees the opposite way. I believe nature has FAR more answers than science. I greatly appreciate the advances in sciences and what it has done to help people, but it has done a considerable deal of harm in not embracing what nature has to offer. When I was a baby, the mothers were told baby formula was far superior than breast milk. Today we know that is completely laughable. But science knows better right? Nope. I worry about science genetically modifying our plants. I understand the idea behind the modification where we make plants to resist all kinds of diseases and bugs, but what is this unnatural food doing to our bodies? We are told by scientists it's perfectly fine. Yeah, that is until we start growing a third leg out of our naval. I don't like that the modified crops pollinate with natural crops and pervert them too. I don't like plugging our livestock with hormones and feeding them unnatural stuff to make them bigger and grow faster. The body wasn't designed that way and I think this is a dangerous trend that could be irreversible.

Well at least look on the positive side- we wouldn't need to worry about global warming since we'll all be dying from some funky disease or cancer because our natural bodies don't know what to do with the mutated food. And as far as global warming is concerned, you have to question its authenticity when scientists keep redefining it, and then have the audacity to insist "the debate is over."

When I was growing up, *Time* magazine had several front cover alarmist articles about global cooling. One of them shows a penguin on top of an iceberg with the words, "How To Survive The Coming Ice Age. 51 Things You Can Do to Make a Difference." Another shows a wide-eyed family huddled together in their home in full winter apparel, sitting around a radiator and watching a tv with the image of a fireplace. The snow outside has huge drifts and the dog inside is shivering under the carpet. The title says "The Cooling of America." There were at least two others that just simply said in big bold letters "THE BIG FREEZE." But *now* we have "global warming." The alarm bells sound again, "DANGER, DANGER, Will Robinson!" Movies are made, actors weep, students wail, songs screech, ex-president wannabes bemoan, "We're doomed" ... But, wait... wait a minute... The computer models have been shown to be bogus and the planet has barely been warming with some meteorologists suggesting that recently it has had no increase or may even slightly be cooling. No problem, we will change the name again to "climate change." That way no matter what happens, cold or warm, we got it covered. This is so preposterous it's hard to fathom that people accept these redefinitions without seeing the agenda behind it. It's like seeing the Wizard of Oz's legs behind the thin curtain, but still thinking the genie is real and you continue believing him. The thing that is crystal clear to me is that there is HUGE money behind this. The debate is not over and qualified people are being silenced. I'm actually not taking a side. If there is a problem, let's honestly talk about it. Let's compare it to the past when we the earth went through wild climate variances when we did not have man-made pollution. Nature has shown a strong resilience to self-correct. I doubt science can do a better job than nature in this correction. The climate change agenda is dubious, but when you try to convince me that cows farting is a colossal problem, I say… "YEAH! DOWN WITH FARTING COWS AND… uh... farting cows… Come again? Haha, you're kidding, right?... No? ... count me out!"

While it seems that there is a global warming agenda, it also seems like there is a pharmaceutical agenda where man-made pills are prescribed rather than nature's cures. I slowly came to the understanding of nature's powerful and effective healing properties that food and herbs provide. A few years ago, my adult son Roman, approached me with a throat full of sores. It was disgusting and I won't describe it 'cause you won't finish reading the book otherwise. I asked him how long it was hurting and he said two weeks. "Two weeks?!" I said, "You should have come to me after three days if it wasn't improving." Since it was evening and I didn't think it was immediately necessary to take him to the emergency room, I made an ole time concoction out of whiskey, honey, lemon and warm water to soothe and heal his throat. I checked the next morning and his throat had significantly improved. He said he felt much better. After two more days, the sores were completely eradicated. My first thought was that there was no medicine I could have purchased in a pharmacy that would have done anything close to what the natural concoction did, and my next thought was more ominous… We are being lied to by science, et al., and the concoctions they foist on us.

This began years of experimentation on myself using natures best. It began with honey, but now includes many other wonderful "products" of nature. I have ONLY personal experimental tests with ZERO medical background, so do your own research. And remember that honey is supposedly unhealthy for infants under twelve months old.

177

Here is what I have learned honey solves so far: almost all throat problems, burns (including sunburn), poison ivy (takes the itch away for much longer than that pink stuff), rashes, acne, and two of the more bizarre ones- pink eye and athlete's foot. I'm still learning. But why should I, a complete science novice, have to learn? Shouldn't this information be so well-known that doctors "prescribe" it? I told customers about my success and many were intrigued. Several did their own tests with the same success. One customer who is a nurse had cellulitis around her eyes. They were swollen and red. She looked like an Irish raccoon. She had the problem for several weeks with no improvement, even though she had spent a small fortune trying to resolve the problem. Since she was a nurse I didn't say anything, but after she expressed exasperation, I told her about my honey experiments. With a, "what do I have to lose" attitude, she applied it around her eyes. The worst that could happen is that you would get sticky… You know, like Tigger said, "YUCK! Tiggers don't like honey- that icky, thticky stuff." The nurse came in several days later, clear-eyed. I asked what happened. She said the honey had cured her in two days.

So my next thought on the homeopathic front was, "What else don't I know?" What other natural stuff out there will cure my ills? I found plenty. I'm still learning and believe I will until I die (hopefully of natural causes rather than a genetically-altered beet; see illustration on opposite page). I think science is coming up to speed on the cures that nature can provide. So while we continue to study "modern medicine," let's put more money and effort into studying nature's medicine. If I, a pleb, have found cures, people with money and scientific skills to study God's creation surely can come up with fantastic natural cures.

beeeet!

Illustrated by Eric England - www.ReapinLizardz.com

There's plenty to appreciate about nature from God's Word. Here are just a few verses:

- *"Through him all things were made; without him nothing was made..."* (John 1:3).

- *"But ask the animals, they will teach you, or the birds in the sky, and they will tell you; or speak to the earth, and it will teach you, or let the fish in the sea inform you. Which of all these of all these does not know that the hand of the LORD has done this? In his hand is the life of every creature and the breath of all mankind,"* (Job 12:7-10).

- *"Let the heavens rejoice, let the earth be glad; let the sea resound, and all that is in it. Let the fields be jubilant, and everything in them; let all the trees of the forest sing for joy,"* (Psalm 96:11-12).

- *"In his hand are the depths of the earth, and the mountains peaks belong to him. The sea is his, for he made it, and his hands formed the dry land,"* (Psalm 95:4-5).

- *"The heavens declare the glory of God; the skies proclaim the work of his hands,"* (Psalm 19:1).

- *"For since the creation of the world God's invisible qualities-his eternal power and divine nature- have been clearly seen, being understood from what has been made, so that people are without excuse,"* (Romans 1:20).

Nature screams out that it was created, while numerous scientists say it just magically happened. If we are, as Dawkins intonates, just DNA dancing to its music, why do we all feel like we are part of this Divine nature? Why, when the deaf hears for the first time, do they cry? Why does one who is colorblind weep for joy when he sees the brilliance of nature's spectacular colors? Why don't they say, "Yeah, whatever." I would argue they are naturally responding to, and inadvertently recognizing, God's created beauty via their new- found senses. If people were only dancing to their DNA, it would seem logical that at least half the people randomly wouldn't care at all about nature, with the other half potentially even hating it. I can hear a spotty few people now saying,

"But, I do hate nature. It's too hot, too cold, too many bugs, too many natural disasters." However there's something *always* wrong for these people. To some extent I agree with them. The something that is always wrong… is them. I recognize that some people who say this *actually* live in harsh environments where food is scarce and daily living is extremely difficult. But this does not mean God's nature is not beautiful, it means you should move to a place more hospitable. It's God's way of saying, "Get thee out of that place. That's for my creepy crawlies, not people…" The rest of us, however, identify with nature's majesty.

God spoke in a loud, dramatic way: nature. He spoke… and it happened. Denying the obvious results of what was spoken into existence is like being the offspring of a king who died when his boy was young. The boy is surrounded by vast wealth including a castle, endless variety of food, priceless paintings and tapestries, highly trained bodyguards to protect him, maids waiting on him hand and foot, and people bowing down to him, giving their money and respect. His father, the king, also recorded his words to him expressing his love for the son, and the king's extensive group of friends all say how great a king he was and relate personal stories of his life and how he raised him. How logical would it be while living amid this all-encompassing opulence, if the king's son concludes, "Yeah, but *I* didn't know him, and he's not speaking to me *now*, so I doubt he ever existed,"? The obvious question to the son would be, "Then where did *you* come from, where did the stuff come from and why are all these people dedicated to you?"

Nature and all its splendor didn't just "happen." It was created for you by a loving God to enjoy together. Just a simple thanks and acknowledgment of Him would do.

11

Life is Harsh

Filthy lies, loneliness, impatience, inadequacy, hypocrisy, drug/alcohol addiction, broken families, suicide, confusion, hatred, laziness, gossips, depression, boredom, physical abuse, slander, arrogance, jealousy, feeling trapped, backstabbing, rage, uncertainty, starvation, ostracism, HOPELESSNESS…

We've all experienced one or many of these problems. We see them every day. We read about them constantly. We live in them and are surrounded by this awfulness. It's the opposite of nature and how God created us to be. We aren't meant for "it" … yet we do it anyway… and we curse ourselves for it… swearing we will never do "that" again… only to do it the next day. Anyone reading this knows that evil exists… and yet participates in it. But we deny the source of this evil.

Satan is the source of life's harshness. Satan HATES you with a burning passion and would love ALL people to suffer, (1 Peter 5:8, 1 John 3:8 & 5:19, 2 Corinthians 4:4, John 10:10, 2 Thessalonians 2:9, 2 Timothy 2:26). His goal is for you to reject God and die, so He can mock God and laughingly say that he destroyed everything precious that God created- especially those who God created in His own image. Satan loves destroying people, destroying minds, crushing marriage and friendships, and causing unspeakable perversions and crimes. We all experience and see it, but we STILL continue with deluded thoughts that there is no FORCE behind this madness.

Satan tempts and most of us listen- giving in to his lies, thereby deeply wounding *ourselves* and the others we are close to, (James 1:14). But we take the easy way out; rather than persevere through the trial, we blame others or God; we quit, run away, pretend, cover up, discard, or continue to hurt ourselves. We ignore the wound until it festers, then we attempt to cover it with a tiny bandage.

Satan loves wreaking havoc. He tried overthrowing God, (Isaiah 14:12-15), but was cast out of heaven. Jesus said, *"I saw Satan fall like lightning out of heaven,"* (Luke 10:18). He is given free reign on earth to cause pain and sorrow if we let him. He travels to and fro throughout the earth like a roaring lion looking for someone to devour, (1 Peter 5:8). He knows how to disguise himself as an angel of light because he once was one, (2 Corinthians 11:14). He already knows that he has lost to Jesus who died for all, and he knows the endgame. So he is trying to do as much damage as he can before the end when God determines it is time to righteously judge the hearts and deeds of all people.

God describes Satan in many ways:

- father of lies (John 8:44)
- cunning serpent (2 Corinthians 11:3)
- great dragon (Revelation 12:9)
- traveler of the world (Ephesians 16:12, Job 1:7)
- has the power of death (Hebrew 2:14)
- prince of the power of air, the spirit in the sons of disobedience (Ephesians 2:2)
- god of this world (2 Corinthians 4:4)
- our adversary (1 Peter 5:8)
- angel of the bottomless pit (Revelation 9:11)
- he ensnares us (2 Timothy 2:26)
- deceiver of the whole world (Revelation 12:9-12)

Satan makes life harsh, but God did not promise an easy life after Adam and Eve betrayed him. They sinned against God just like we all do today. But God gives us a free way out through Christ, (John 3:16-21). Christians cannot defeat Satan but we can make him flee, (James 4:7). Christians fall to the Deceiver's power because they *let* him (James 1:14-15). In fact, Christians might be the most susceptible to his deceit because we are Satan's primary targets. He knows God's Word and twists it just enough to deceive believers who, despicably, don't know God's Word or how to defend against his attacks. So they commit unspeakable acts, sometimes in the name of God, for the world to see, and as a result of their ignorance, chase people from the Truth. No one escapes Satan's touch. When Jesus was on the verge of starvation He had to endure Satan's attacks, but did not listen to his lies or let him have rule over Him, (Matthew 4:1-11). Satan aggressively attacks Christians specifically because he already has the non-believer in his grasp, or has fooled the non-believer into believing that he doesn't even exist.

To guard against his stealthy lies, we need to ALWAYS be vigilant, and ALWAYS on guard:

- *"By this it is evident who are the children of God, and who are the children of the devil: whoever does not practice righteousness is not of God, nor is the one who does not love his brother,"* (1 John 3:10).

- *"Submit yourselves, then, to God. Resist the devil, and he will flee from you,"* (James 4:7).

- *"Do not give the devil a foothold,"* (Ephesians 4:27).

- *"For the law of the Spirit of life in Christ Jesus has set me free from the law of sin and death,"* (Romans 8:2).

- *"Put on the full armor of God,"* (Ephesians 6:10-18).

These verses show Satan is on the hunt to kill and destroy and that we need to defend against him in all ways. His attacks remind me of a simple analogy when I played paintball with my friends; We were a ragtag bunch of first time paintballers out to have some goofy fun. We were placed against a bunch of dudes with their own equipment that looked like they spent all day polishing and customizing. I'm a proficient shot, but I figured we were going to get annihilated. So instead of trying to take them head on, I tried stealthily hiding and pot-shotting them. I looked under the barricades that they were hiding behind which was only two inches off the ground. I was about twenty yards away and aimed for the only part of a person I could see- a guy's foot. I aimed and shot. He hopped and screamed, "OW, WHO THE HELL SHOT ME IN THE FOOT?" I laughed for the next ten minutes. Actually, I'm still laughing as I type this, so I guess I've been laughing for about twenty years.

I relate that simple story to warn people who think they may be in a safe spot, that you cannot hide from Satan. If he has no other shot, he will hit you in the foot. Whatever you leave exposed, he will hit. When you don't pay attention to God or His Word to protect yourself... Satan pounces. This is why the Christian church and its leaders often fail- because pastors, bishops and church members, drop their guard. They don't pray, fast, read, study His Word, or sharpen each other by debating God's Word. They don't deny themselves and take up the cross every day, (Luke 9:23). They don't place ALL their thoughts captive to Christ, (2 Corinthians 10:5). They don't strive for perfection, (Matthew 5:48). They don't protect themselves by putting on the FULL armor of God, (Ephesians 6:10-18). They ALLOW themselves to be overcome! (Matthew 12:45, Romans 6:1-11)

Satan hates everyone, all of God's creation. He will not take a break from attacking us, so we cannot take a break from defending. When we die, he will stand next to us in heaven and accuse us of our sin, both day and night! (Revelations 12:9-12, Zechariah 3:1). And unfortunately, he will be right. However, those who have accepted Jesus have conquered Satan and have been set free from their guilt. Jesus will step in and say to Satan, "He/She is mine. He/She is pardoned." Romans 8:1-39 sums it up:

What then shall we say to these things? If God is for us, who can be against us? He who did not spare his own Son but gave him up for us all, how will he not also with him graciously give us all things? Who shall bring any charge against God's elect? It is God who justifies. Who is to condemn? Christ Jesus is the one who died—more than that, who was raised—who is at the right hand of God, who indeed is interceding for us. Who shall separate us from the love of Christ? Shall tribulation, or distress, or persecution, or famine, or nakedness, or danger, or sword? As it is written, "For your sake we are being killed all the day long; we are regarded as sheep to be slaughtered." No, in all these things we are more than conquerors through him who loved us. For I am sure that neither death nor life, nor angels nor rulers, nor things present nor things to come, nor powers, nor height nor depth, nor anything else in all creation, will be able to separate us from the love of God in Christ Jesus our Lord.

12

God is Dead?

"God Is Dead."
-Friedrich Nietzsche

I'm guessing that was news to God... now Nietzsche knows better.

This was the chapter I was most apprehensive to write. What could I possibly say about God? "He's... uh... big! Yeah, big... and... STRONG! He can leap tall buildings in a single bound! What's that? ..That's Superman you say? Get outta here... I'm sure it's in the Bible."

What could I possibly say that God hasn't already said or shown? ..Nothing.

God shows us that He is science and nature through what He created. Everything works within the laws that He has established. Science uses our minds through God's laws to try and explain the unknown, while nature nurtures our souls and puts us into commune with His majesty. We know it innately, but either choose to ignore or discredit it. He created our senses to see, hear, smell, taste and feel the essence of His magnificence. If you let your stubborn self go, you will experience His love.

Can we prove God? I've heard this from non-Christians innumerable times. "Where is He? Introduce Him to me. I've never seen Him," ...they unintelligently mock. If this dumb "logic" is insisted on, then I would ask the non-Christian a similar question- prove to me that something comes from nothing. Show me thought. Show me love. Show me fear. You can't- only symptoms of them. "Give" the non-Christian *nothing* and tell him to make *something* from it. Both sides can play this insipid argument. I had a similar verbal exchange with a college student named Sarah several years ago:

My friend Eric and I were in the art building at Kent State talking about life, with the immediate subject being Jesus. Eric was sculpting and I his studly model. The art building was filled with all sorts of proudly odd and unique individuals. As Eric and I bantered, we were stealthily overheard by Sarah, a lady of refinement (in her own unique way), with real bones sticking out of her long, unkempt, dyed black hair. (Not kidding and no, I did not inquire as to the critter the bones came from.) She came out of hiding in the balcony and screeched through her black lipsticked mouth, "If I could prove to you that Jesus didn't exist would you believe me?" Eric and I answered differently. He said no and I said yes. Eric understandably answered with what he truly believed. But I thought her question was a trap to show how unyielding Christians are even if the evidence, as Sarah put it, was… PROOF. So instead of answering what I believed, I listened to HER. She said "if" she could "prove." Then of course, yes, I must believe her. I asked her to come down and engage in the conversation, which she did. I loved talking to Sarah with her full, thick, raccoon-emulating, black mascara-encircled eyes. She had an interesting perspective on everything. I reversed her question and asked, "If I could prove Jesus was true, would you believe me?" She quickly shot back that everything was relative and nervously ended the conversation. Sarah avoided me for the next two years.

You see, Sarah tried to usurp our conversation and show the pettines of Christians who often constrain themselves by their own thoughts and traditions. But, if we just simply listen without presupposition, we can relate heart to heart instead of theory to theory. Neither of us can prove God in a concrete way, but we can try in an empirical way. I believe the empirical evidence is overwhelmingly in God's favor.

As established, it is not possible to argue all the points in God's favor in this book. But I will address a few major sticking points that have caused people not to believe in God. One of these would be the difference between a so-called angry Old Testament God and a loving New Testament God. The initial accusation seems fair. There are numerous verses that establish God's Old Testament wrath. If we look at the "law book" of Leviticus 20:1-27, it's all about the Levitical law and its penalty, which often is death.

- 2 "'...who sacrifices any of his children to Molek is to be put to death.'"

- 9 "'Anyone who curses their father or mother is to be put to death.'"

- 10 "'If a man commits adultery with another man's wife... both the adulterer and the adulteress are to be put to death.'"

- 13 "'If a man has sexual relations with a man as one does with a woman, both of them have done what is detestable. They are to be put to death...'"

- 15 "'If a man has sexual relations with an animal, he is to be put to death, and you must kill the animal.'"

- 22 "'Keep all my decrees and laws and follow them, so that the land where I am bringing you to live may not vomit you out. You must not live according to the customs of the nations I am going *to drive out before you. Because they did all these things, I abhorred them... I am the Lord your God, who has set you apart from the nations.'"*

- *27 "'A man or woman who is a medium or spiritist among you must be put to death. You are to stone them; their blood will be on their own heads.'"*

And then here is the loving New Testament God as illustrated in 1 John 4:7-19;

- *7 "...love comes from God. Everyone who loves has been born of God and knows God."*

- *8 "...God is love."*

- *10 "..not that we loved God, but that he loved..."*

- *11 "Dear friends, since God so loved us..."*

- *12 "...his love is made complete in us."*

- *16 "...God is love..."*

- *19 "...he first loved us."*

On closer inspection, we see this "cherry-picking" texts because it can be reversed. Here also is the loving God in the Old Testament:

- *God created a perfect world for us; God saw all that he had made, and it was very good,* (Genesis 1:31).

- *He created us IN HIS OWN IMAGE!* (Genesis 1:27).

- *He completely provided for us with food,* (Genesis 1:29), *and even sewed our clothes after we betrayed him,* (Genesis 3:21).

- *The Lord is slow to anger and abounding in love and faithfulness,* (Exodus 34:6; Numbers 14:18; Deuteronomy 4:31; Nehemiah 9:17; Psalm 86:5, 15; 108:4; 145:8; Joel 2:13).

I could list hundreds of verses of His love, protection and provision from the Old Testament. So what about an angry New Testament God? Jesus, being God's representative in the New Testament said:

- *"...if you do not forgive others their sins, your Father will not forgive your sins,"* (Matthew 6:15).

- *"...whoever disowns me before others, I will disown before my Father in heaven,"* (Matthew 10:33-34).

- *"Vengeance is mine,"* Romans (12:19).

- *"The Son of Man will send out his angels, and they will weed out of his kingdom everything that causes sin and all who do evil. They will throw them into the blazing furnace, where there will be weeping and gnashing of teeth,"* Matthew (13:41-42).

- *"...brood of vipers, hypocrites, snakes..."* (Matthew 12:34).

- *"Get behind me Satan,"* (Matthew 16:23).

- *"...no one is good, not even one,"* (Romans 3:12).

So why does it SEEM like there is a difference? Simply, because of Jesus. He paid the final price for all the Law and the prophets (Romans 3:21-26). Before Jesus, there was the Law that had specific and harsh punishments, but the ultimate punishment never changed. The punishment from the start (after sin) was death. Genesis 2:17 says, *"...you must not eat from the tree of the knowledge of good and evil, for when you eat from it you will certainly die."* This still applies today. Romans 6:23 says, *"For the wages of sin is death, but the gift of God is eternal life in Christ Jesus our Lord."* The difference then is only *perceived.* If you look at the whole Bible, God is consistent.

This brings up another issue that I hear often. Christopher Hitchens called God the Celestial Dictator, or worse, a genocidal maniac, and though I understand his sentiments, I completely disagree. Christopher points out that God called for some groups of people to be completely annihilated- men, women, children and animals, (1 Samuel 15:3). On the face of it, it sounds like Hitchens' "genocidal maniac" God theory would be correct. There are lots of examples of death and destruction in the Bible. If you think this makes a case for an evil God, you are one-dimensionally sighted. You can only see things from your limited human brain with worldly ethics and then place them on a God who has no such restrictions. But, if there is a God, He knows the hearts and minds of all people. He would know if they are evil. Nobody else could possibly know this. If God exists, and He made us, and we continually betray Him, it is His total right to wipe EVERYBODY out if He so chose. But in this 1 Samuel example, the Amalekites who were all put to death may have been some of the most immoral people who ever lived. If there were a group of bloodthirsty people on earth today who raped, slaughtered, chopped off heads and demanded that all mankind do as they say, we would want to wipe them off the face of the earth! Let's say we could see into their hearts and minds and we KNEW they would not change. Then it would seem good, right and fair to wipe them off the face of the earth, and I doubt anyone today would be against that. Well, God DOES know these things and when HE acts knowingly and righteously we scream, "HE'S A MANIAC!" It's laughable.

As stated in many places elsewhere in this book, the Christian church has committed grim atrocities in the name of Christ. But understand that phraseology, "in the NAME of Christ"… it was not in the SPIRIT of Christ. The Catholic Inquisition was hellishly wrong, just like the Muslim head-choppers are today. Jesus' words spoke in direct contradiction to the atrocities carried out in His name. So indeed, they really can't be called "Christian" since they went *against* Christ's teachings. Non-Christians often use these atrocities committed in the name of Christ as an excuse not to believe. I would heartily agree if they were using it as a reason not to believe in PEOPLE, but they are using deranged people to not believe in God. Non-believers continue by saying that Christianity has killed more people in the world than anybody. Here I call BS. Frankly, I don't think the groups that committed these crimes were Christians. But, most of the genocidal maniacs PROHIBITED people to believe in God or ruled from a warped religious understanding: Stalin (Russia), Hitler (Germany), Pol Pot (Cambodia), Mao Zedong (China), Yakubu Gowon (Nigeria), Mengistu Haile Mariam (Ethiopia), Kim Il Sung (North Korea), Ismail Enver Pasha (Turkey, Ottoman Empire), Hideki Tojo (Japan), and Leopoldo II (Belgium). And for dishonorable mention: Mugabe, Vlad the Impaler, Kim Jong Il, Idi Amin, Lenin, Hirohito, Brezhnev, Chiang Kai-sheik, Kaiser Wilhelm II, and Ho Chi Minh. We must be careful in rejecting God based on the horrors perpetrated by evil people.

So I say to all you naysayers and bobbleheads; Try and prove to yourself that God doesn't exist; that the Bible is false. Take the challenge.

But don't look only to the biased sources to back-up the point that you already believe- compare it with the Christian arguments. C.S. Lewis set out to do just that. He was positive he could "disprove" God. Through an intellectually honest endeavor, he ended up proving God to himself and continued to support his beliefs through writing numerous books such as *The Chronicles of Narnia, The Screwtape Letters*, or *Mere Christianity.* Lee Strobel, (*The Case for Christ* or *The Case for a Creator*) and Josh McDowell, who authored or co-authored over 100 books (*Evidence that Demands a Verdict*, or *More Than a Carpenter*), also set out to disprove God and ended the same way as CS Lewis. Read their books and refute them if you can! There are numerous other intellectuals who traveled the same road of unbelief until they honestly delved into the evidence. Listen to people like Ravi Zacharias and his team, especially his Q&As, and see if you can counter their answers.

In fact, let me ask the naysayers some questions. If the Bible is false, then who wrote it? How did it get compiled? How can this great conspiracy have been *coordinated* OVER THOUSANDS OF YEARS, and why?- for brainwashing? It doesn't make sense. If you intend to control people or get them to believe in your "myth," you would write the decrees and laws DURING that time period, NOT have the writing spread out over thousands of years, written by dozens of people. How does one coherently write a book that can last thousands of years with all the cultural shifts and it *still* be relevant today for everyday living? Why does archeology continue PROVING the Bible as they keep unearthing artifacts? And most importantly, why would a book trying to fool people KILL OFF its main character? Go after these questions. Try to prove your conspiracy theory. I double dare you.

While you try to disprove God, let me give you some factual evidence about Jesus and his life… from the OLD TESTAMENT! As mentioned in chapter nine, the Dead Sea Scrolls were found in 1947 and contained tens of thousands of parts of the Old Testament. These fragments were scientifically dated to hundreds of years *PRIOR* to Jesus being born. Unlike scientific theories, these are facts. This is called prophecy. There is no logical way for this to be dismissed. I have read several illogical attempts, however. Here are some highlights of the Old Testament verses that predate Jesus by hundreds of years and when he fulfilled them.

- *"The virgin will be with child and will give birth to a son, and will call him Immanuel,"* (Isaiah 7:14; fulfilled Matt 1:22-24).

- *"For to us a child is born, to us a son is given, and the government will be on his shoulders. And he will be called Wonderful Counselor, Mighty God, Everlasting Father, Prince of Peace,"* (Isaiah 9:6; fulfilled Luke 2:11).

- *"Rejoice greatly, O Daughter of Zion! Shout, Daughter of Jerusalem! See, your king comes to you, righteous and having salvation, gentle and riding on a donkey, on a colt, the foal of a donkey,"* (Zechariah 9:9; fulfilled Mark 11:7-11).

- *"But you, Bethlehem Ephrathah, though you are small among the clans of Judah, out of you will come for me one who will be ruler over Israel, whose origins are from of old, from ancient times,"* (Micah 5:2; fulfilled Matt 2:1).

- *"Dogs have surrounded me; a band of evil men has encircled me, they have pierced my hands and my feet. I can count all my bones; people stare and gloat over me. They divide my garments among them and cast lots for my clothing,"* (Psalm 22:16-18; fulfilled John 19). This was several hundred years before Christ was born, describing a type of execution that did not exist at the time!

- The entire fifty-third chapter of Isaiah. Isaiah 53:3-7 is especially unmistakable in its description of Jesus:

    He was despised and rejected by men, a man of sorrows, and familiar with suffering. Like one from whom men hide their faces he was despised, and we esteemed him not. Surely he took up our infirmities and carried our sorrows, yet we considered him stricken by God, smitten by him, and afflicted. But he was pierced for our transgressions, he was crushed for our iniquities; the punishment that brought us peace was upon him, and by his wounds we are healed. We all, like sheep, have gone astray, each of us has turned to his own way; and the LORD has laid on him the iniquity of us all. He was oppressed and afflicted, yet he did not open his mouth; he was led like a lamb to the slaughter, and as a sheep before her shearers is silent, so he did not open his mouth.

- The price that was paid for Jesus to be betrayed, *"I told them, 'If you think it best, give me my pay; but if not, keep it.' So they paid me thirty pieces of silver. And the Lord said to me, 'Throw it to the potter'—the handsome price at which they valued me! So I took the thirty pieces of silver and threw them to the potter at the house of the Lord,"* (Zechariah 11:12-13; fulfilled in Matt 27:9-10).

- *"I offered my back to those who beat me, my cheeks to those who pulled out my beard; I did not hide my face from mocking and spitting,"* (Isaiah 50:6; fulfilled Matt 26.67, John 19:1)

- *"They put gall in my food and gave me vinegar for my thirst,"* (Psalm 69:21; fulfilled Matt 27:34).

- Even John the Baptist was prophesied about in preparing the way of the Lord: *"A voice of one calling in the wilderness: 'Prepare the way for the Lord; make straight in the desert a highway for our God,'"* (Isaiah 40:3, fulfilled Matt 3:1-3).

Jesus is the stumbling block for all of us. Only a very tiny number of people claim that He isn't real. The vast majority of scholars say there is no doubt He lived the life that is claimed in the Bible. There are plenty of excellent books from antiquity to today that support this claim. The Muslims said some six hundred years *after* Jesus was crucified that he didn't really die on the cross, but within thirty to forty years of his suffering and death it was recorded that He did indeed die. Show me the EVIDENCE that He didn't... not your opinion... evidence. I'll save you some time. There isn't any.

I heard people say they don't believe in Jesus because it's dumb that God would sacrifice His only Son this way. "Why would God do that?" I find this argument peculiar and sad. When we read a person sacrificed themselves to save another, we call them a hero. When Jesus did that for us, you call it dumb! If someone were to die in place of all the wrong crap that we have done in our lives, it only makes sense it would be THE person that NEVER did wrong crap! And don't say it was easy for Him not to sin since He was God. The Bible says Jesus was fully man and fully God, (Hebrews 2:17, John 10:30). While on Earth He was fully man. Then how did He do all those miracles? He said it was God working through Him and He could do nothing on His own, (John 5:19). Critics then use that point to say He could then do nothing, therefore He could not be God. Aha checkmate! Not so. Jesus was man on Earth which is why God had to work through Him. After He lived a tortuous life on Earth without sinning and then died, He took on all the attributes of God. He said, *"I and the Father are one,"* (John 10:30). And again I ask, "Why would a bunch of guys write a book where they want to fool the public, by killing off the main character?"

God's Word is THE authority about life and has every answer to all problems. Not everything is recorded in the Bible, only what is needed to live a life pleasing to Him. Why doesn't God tell us the EXACT details of His world and show Himself to us to save a lot of pain? He wanted us to be directly involved. He wanted us to figure out relationships and how to love His way. He wanted us to overcome difficulties by using His world and His Word. He wanted us to find the elements He placed into the ground and air, to eventually figure out how to make a tire, or the particle accelerator Hadron Collider. He wants us to engage our brains, to find stuff, to figure out what to do with it. How enjoyable would a treasure hunt be if you were told where the prize was? A simple acknowledgment of His spectacular creation would be nice, like- "Thanks God." Or even a reverent "WHOA" would suffice. God would understand and appreciate the sentiment, (Malachi 3:16-17).

God created all, ESPECIALLY YOU. He fashioned nature with His words for your pleasure and well-being. He gave you freedom to accept OR reject Him so you wouldn't be a puppet.

God doesn't owe you anything. He's given all and paid it all.

God is the Alpha and the Omega.

God is Love.

13

Believe

We are all in this soup together- Life Soup. Each of us have our special contributions to its remarkable flavoring. Without all the ingredients working together it tastes odd and incomplete. When even the most simple component is missing, you know something is just not right, but you don't know what or why. When rancid products are added, the whole taste suffers, or too much of any one thing, and it begins to be bland. If the vegetables had a coup and said there was no need for the broth, it wouldn't be soup- it would be a bunch of vegetables lying in the bottom of a pot. Then the vegetables would likely start a power struggle between all the individual parts, sadly leading to an ingredient war, rather than the intended delicious soup. If each ingredient thought it was the most important and imposed itself on the soup, we'd have something that tasted and looked like dirt. When the soup seems all but lost, the ingredients agree to tolerate each other but don't want to associate while they blame each other for the now non-soup. As each ingredient proudly and defiantly sits there on the counter, they look up at the bemused soup maker, blame him for their individual plight, and say, "What's the matter with you? Why can't you make a tasty soup?!"

This is life in a soup pot. We are all in it together and should be adding to the world's flavor. But we are too egocentric to see past ourselves in what others have to contribute to the world. We blame other ingredients and ultimately the Soup Maker. So we go rancid.

This is why decades ago, I decided to add to the spice of life. To seek the best Soup Maker and recipe for life. Then to follow the recipe and love people as God asked me to. To share in an earthy, natural way what He has shown me. Do I like the heat that I have gone through? No and Yes. I certainly don't like it when going through it and have often complained bitterly, but now appreciate the lessons taught. I'm still learning, but now a more willing student.

I implore the reader to reconsider the God of Jesus based on His Word and His creations. PLEASE do not look at Christians to see if this God is real. As the title says... they "suck." We hypocritically do not love properly and present a bad example of what is good and perfect.

Christians, we need to love better and understand there is only one true definition of love and then diligently practice it. More people would care what we had to say if we listened without condemning. Some people will continue to be belligerent to your love, like the hostility they showed Jesus by torturing and hanging Him on a cross. Since we believe to have the truth of God's Word, we should know better... so be better.

Let's end the madness of this world. Let's stop participating in its insanity and start improving it one person at a time, starting with YOU. Stop playing God by living by your own rules, and be the person He knows you can be by playing by His rules. Don't try to get good before you get God. God will help you get good. End your personal struggle and torture, and turn your life over to the only One who can erase your past and give you peace. For you who lost your faith in God, reconsider. For you who never had faith, please consider it. For you who believe other faiths, please examine all the evidence on your own and ask the true God to reveal Himself to you. We are here for a reason and that reason is not "chance."

For those who want to know this loving God, ask Him. He requires nothing fancy... only you. Your biggest "crime" is not loving the One who created you. Acknowledge Him and He will acknowledge you. *"Come, all who are weary, and He will give you rest,"* (Matthew 11:28), and find a *"peace that passes all understanding,"* (Philippians 4:7). Jesus is the way, the truth, and the life, (John 14:6). He came to seek and save the lost and hurting, (Luke 19:10). He lived perfectly yet suffered an excruciating death in your place, so that you may be completely forgiven. When you repent and believe, you will be unconditionally set free from your personal bondage. Problems will still occur, but you will have a new, hope-filled way of seeing and dealing with them. The Holy Spirit enthusiastically waits to enter you upon your decision. Confess in your heart that Jesus died for you and that God raised Him from the grave, and you will live in eternal love forever.

Be a rebel: do good, pursue truth, and... love.

Addendum 1
(From Chapter 5- Christians... meh)

Bible study synopsis of resolving disputes between believers:

-God's word is not complicated
-God's word is THE authority and has every answer to all problems.
-This is NOT legal advice. This is God's Word (the LAW of God), which is better than legal advice.

Here is where it is evident that the Christian church is failing:
-As a Christian body, we are an embarrassment and mockery to Jesus and our Creator when the church statistics in "crimes against God" are nearly the same in secular society- i.e. divorce, out-of-wedlock births, adultery, law suits, etc. What message does this send to the world?

-The church is afraid (legally?) and/or unwilling to tackle difficult, (for those involved, but not for God,) problems and often lets their congregation destroy each other in secular courts, (by not properly intervening).

Moses and our Lord knew this and set up a "judgeship":

Exodus 18:13-26:

   13 *The next day Moses took his seat to serve as judge for the people, and they stood*

around him from morning till evening. 14 When his father-in-law saw all that Moses

was doing for the people, he said, "What is this you are doing for the people? Why do

you alone sit as judge, while all these people stand around you from morning till

evening?"

15 Moses answered him, *"Because the people come to me to seek God's will. 16 Whenever they have a dispute, it is brought to me, and I decide between the parties and inform them of God's decrees and laws."*

17 Moses' father-in-law replied, *"What you are doing is not good. 18 You and these people who come to you will only wear yourselves out. The work is too heavy for you; you cannot handle it alone. 19 Listen now to me and I will give you some advice, and may God be with you. You must be the people's representative before God and bring their disputes to him. 20 Teach them the decrees and laws, and show them the way to live and the duties they are to perform. 21 But select capable men from all the people—men who fear God, trustworthy men who hate dishonest gain—and appoint them as officials over thousands, hundreds, fifties and tens. 22 Have them serve as judges for the people at all times, but have them bring every difficult case to you; the simple cases they can decide themselves. That will make your load lighter, because they will share it with you. 23 If you do this and God so commands, you will be able to stand the strain, and all these people will go home satisfied."*

24 Moses listened to his father-in-law and did everything he said. 25 He chose capable men from all Israel and made them leaders of the people, officials over thousands, hundreds, fifties and tens. 26 They served as judges for the people at all times. The difficult cases they brought to Moses, but the simple ones they decided themselves.

-It is a travesty and mockery of the Christian faith when the body of Christ suffers and we say, "God be with you," instead of assisting in resolving the problems and pains.

1 Corinthians 12:12-26:
"...so that there should be no division in the body, but that its parts should have equal concern for each other. 26 If one part suffers, every part suffers with it..."

-Here's an analogy: if a beautiful house has a broken sewer pipe in the basement, the whole house will stink.

God does not take sueing each other in secular courts lightly. It not only puts the individual Christian on trial, it puts Christianity on trial. No matter what the outcome, Christianity loses.

Corinthians 6:1-8:

1 If any of you has a dispute with another, dare he take it before the ungodly for judgment instead of before the saints? 2 Do you not know that the saints will judge the world? And if you are to judge the world, are you not competent to judge trivial cases? 3 Do you not know that we will judge angels? How much more the things of this life! 4 Therefore, if you have disputes about such matters, appoint as judges even men of little account in the church! 5 I say this to shame you. Is it possible that there is nobody among you wise enough to judge a dispute between believers? 6 But instead, one brother goes to law against another—and this in front of unbelievers!

7 The very fact that you have lawsuits among you means you have been completely defeated already. Why not rather be wronged? Why not rather be cheated? 8 Instead, you yourselves cheat and do wrong, and you do this to your brothers.

-The church should have a system and people in place to decide these matters.

-The people placed into this "judgeship" should be proven to display love, wisdom and a useful understanding of God's word.

-The Bible gives an outline of the process:

Matthew 5:22-24:

22 But I tell you that anyone who is angry with his brother will be subject to judgment. Again, anyone who says to his brother, 'Raca' is answerable to the Sanhedrin. But anyone who says, 'You fool!' will be in danger of the fire of hell.

23 "Therefore, if you are offering your gift at the altar and there remember that your brother has something against you, 24 leave your gift there in front of the altar. First go and be reconciled to your brother; then come and offer your gift.

Matthew 18:15-17:

> *15 "If your brother sins against you, go and show him his fault, just between the two of you. If he listens to you, you have won your brother over. 16 But if he will not listen, take one or two others along, so that 'every matter may be established by the testimony of two or three witnesses.' 17 If he refuses to listen to them, tell it to the church; and if he refuses to listen even to the church, treat him as you would a pagan or a tax collector.*

-This proposed system applies to believers and those within the Christian church structure.

1 Corinthians 5:12-13:

> *12 What business is it of mine to judge those outside the church? Are you not to judge those inside? 13 God will judge those outside. "Expel the wicked man from among you."*

-This process should not fall on the deacons' and elders' shoulders who are already overburdened, but those deemed worthy to carry out such a system by the church.

Addendum 2
(From Chapter 6- My Answer is No)

This is a raw email exchange between two believers on the subject of marriage. We are both searching for the truth- but disagree. It is healthy for Christians to engage in debates. God's word says we sharpen each other this way, (Proverbs 27:17). "Paul" disagrees with my premise that the sexual union IS the marriage. His email is first and then comes my reply. (The emails are not corrected for grammar.)

"Paul's" email:

Marriage --- A Christian View

Sorry about the delay – as you mentioned – life gets in the way.
Thus, we begin –I think that the only question that I will try and address here deals with the premarital sexual permission that is/will be/has been given to a young couple prior to their wedding day (and night).
Posed as follows : 'Should this young couple (if currently chaste) have sex the night prior to their wedding?' (if not chaste – another discussion).
-- My strong heartfelt recommendation is – Absolutely Not!
Why not – The reasons are myriad and are as follows:
. The Jewish system of marriage consisted of a lengthy betrothal period whereby the bride & groom were already committed (even considered fully married) to one another. Mary & Joseph would fit this example as Joseph upon hearing of Mary's pregnancy resolved to divorce her quietly. As we know, Mary was a virgin (even though betrothed to

Joseph), they had no conjugal relations until after Jesus was born, and they certainly did after that.

There is NO similar situation in America today. We may say that a couple is 'engaged', but there is no legal ramification (or church discipline situation for that matter) that ensues once an engagement is broken; whereas, in Jewish culture the betrothal period was considered legally binding. Thus, in some ways, the 2 systems (that in Ancient Jewish tradition & that of the Church in America today) are not directly comparable but we can certainly draw some scriptural parallels.

Back to Mary & Joseph, it begs the question....why did they NOT have relations when they were betrothed? After all, in accord with the reasoning that they could be considered married, why not consummate their relationship (being betrothed was more certain than being engaged). It is due to the fact, that although committed, they awaited the fulfillment of the 'ketubbah' contract (1st marriage stage) when they could have sexual relations with one another (2nd stage- 'chuppah'). The wedding 'feast' (3rd stage) did indeed follow the consummation of the marriage but the case to be made is that they were fully married at the TIME when the marriage contract was agreed to ! A certificate of divorce would have to be written and legally completed (during stage 1) even if there was NO sexually activity. Thus, the ONLY time where our current marital tradition could intersect the Jewish tradition would be where the marriage contract becomes binding (at the altar on any American couple's wedding day). At that time, they would be somewhat in 'sync', if you will, and could consummate their marriage.

The wedding feast was rooted in a biblical understanding of marriage and there was no "wedding ceremony" in the synagogue in the first century, performed under a canopy where the bride and groom would hold hands and say, "I do" before an audience of friends and family. This didn't develop for hundreds of years after Jesus death, burial and resurrection.

2. I wanted to make it clear that I also hold to a couple of positions that are traditionally outside of a regular Orthodox Christian Worldview. As that is the case, I have to seriously evaluate my thinking in light of what I know to be true in other plain scriptural cases, and ask myself the question – 'Am I missing something & will I appear before the King of Kings and have him ask me, 'Why did you not believe ?' So this always causes me to pause & evaluate where I may be off base. One may say that Martin Luther or John Calvin challenged the normative Christian Worldview and I would heartily agree, but I would also mention to them that – 'I ain't no' Martin Luther (and I expect that you would agree to this in your case?!?).

Our pastor mentioned in church today that a seminary student at RPTS in Wilkinsburg mentioned to a professor that he found a 'new' position not identified in 17 differing well-respected commentaries. The professor said, 'Son –tear up your paper and begin again.' The premise that he found something 'new' which was not yet clearly articulated by our spiritual fathers or accepted was not a satisfactory premise to the professor.

Brad, I would encourage to ask yourself – is my counsel 'off track?'

3. God presided at the first wedding (Gen 2:21-25, below), and the current wedding ceremony invokes God to author, bless, sanctify, watch, and keep any marriage in which He is called upon. I would submit that the wedding ceremony is the time & place where any current marriage is fully united by the Father, Son and Holy Ghost, and therefore I would NOT encourage any couple to engage in any sexual activity prior to this time.

'What God has joined together, let no man put asunder'

So the LORD God caused the man to fall into a deep sleep; and while he was sleeping, he took one of the man's ribs and closed up the place with flesh. Then the LORD God made a woman from the rib he had taken out of the man, and he brought her to the man. The man said, "This is now

bone of my bones and flesh of my flesh; she shall be called 'woman, ' for she was taken out of man." For this reason a man will leave his father and mother and be united to his wife, and they will become one flesh. The man and his wife were both naked, and they felt no shame.
As you wrestle with this, let me leave you with the words of Melanchthon:
In essentials, unity; in differences, liberty; in all things, charity. (I believe that this serves all believers well)
Blessings, Paul. (Paul then gave several websites to back up his point of view- which are not listed here)

Brad's response:
Hey Paul,
Very nice of you to write. I appreciate you thinking about this matter.

I too looked in depth at the subject and I am all the more convinced of the position that the sexual union between a man and a woman IS the marriage.

The greek word for betrothed as in Matthew 1:18 is mnésteuó. It means " I ask in marriage" or espouse or promised. Notice in the same verse it says; "...Mary had been betrothed to Joseph, BEFORE THEY CAME TOGETHER...". This is bolstering the very point I believe God is making and I am postulating.

I agree with your assessment of the Jewish marriage tradition. Betrothal was/is an important step in the marriage process but IT IS NOT marriage. This process was so important in those days that Joseph even commented he would give Mary a certificate of "divorce" (vs 19),... or did he? It would seem obvious that they were already "married" otherwise why would a divorce certificate be needed? Well, it wasn't. The actual greek words say; "...eboulethe lathra apolysai auten..." or "...purposed secretly to send away her..." There is no mention of a certificate and in this case "divorce" is used synonymously as "separate from" or "send away"- not divorce in the sense that society knows it today.

However having said this I also believe God is saying that an agreement (or betrothal, or in today's lexicon- engaged, or biblically- choosing to leave) is a big part of the marriage process, but the physical sexual union is the consummation of that marriage.

All the more telling is the fact that there are no biblical examples of any church or state authorities being involved in the marriage.

Also, just because something is a tradition does not necessarily make it right. God's word trumps tradition. Indeed I would argue that it is BECAUSE we have allowed church tradition to reign that we have lost sight of God's word and His truth. Tradition is not bad UNLESS it trumps God's word. Then it is evil. Jesus excoriates the traditionalists of his time. Matthew 23:13-33.

I disagree with your Martin Luther suggestions. ANYONE is a "Martin Luther" if they stand against church tradition accurately using the word of God. I thank God for the future Martin Luther's' and look forward to a spirit-lead interpretation of God's word. To say that no more Martin Luther's' are needed is stating the church has it all correct now. If this is true I would like to know which church that is so I can become a member.

Also I disagree with your professor example of tearing up a thesis because the student said he has a new way. That is arrogant (a definition of hate) of the professor to immediately assume the student is wrong. Let the student write the paper and then point out that idea was already proposed by so-n-so. If this type of thinking were truly implemented in life there would be no new ideas or inventions.

I looked at some of the resource links that you supplied. Most have to do with ancient jewish tradition. I looked at the 9 Focus on the Family articles by Dr. David Kyle Foster and found them more extensive and wordy than God's own word. It also lacks biblical verses to back up his points. So mainly it's just another persons viewpoint rather than God's. This is one of the points I am trying to make in this book. Let's stop yapping and start quoting God's word. He said it best and doesn't need anyone adding to his word.

Finally I did an exhaustive hebrew and greek bible study on all the words referring to marriage, married, marry, wed, wedding, wedded etc. What I found was fascinating and I believe solidly fortifies my postulation on marriage.

Biblically there is a distinct difference between "marriage" and "wedding". I found 19 hebrew and greek words for marriage, most of which are referring to a physical connection, union or sexual duty. There are only 3 words for wedding and two of those are only used once each in the old testament. The new testament references to a wedding such as the one you referred to at Cana (John 2:1-12) are all one word; gamos which in the cases that it is used means wedding celebration. It is used 13 times 8 of which are in Matthew 22:2-12, otherwise it is only used 5 other times.

The study I did is 11 pages long all with Strong's reference numbers and notes. It is very cool and miraculous that we can study from the original sources of God's word.

Here are some of the verses that I mentioned when you were in the store that support this viewpoint. I have about 80 additional verses that also would lend support.

**A very important note to all the verses is that they are all about the sexual union in relationship to being a wife and have NOTHING to do with a ceremony or anyone else involved.

Abraham takes Sarah's maid (Hagar) as a wife; Gen 16:2-4 The hebrew words say, "...nathan eth Abram enosh low ishshah bo el Hagar harah...", which translates; "...and gave her Abram another to him as wife And he went in unto Hagar and she conceived..."

Abraham and Keturah (wife after Sarah dies) Gen 25:1 The hebrew words say, "...yasaph Abraham laqach ishshah shem Keturah yalad eth...", which translates "...Then again Abraham also took a wife and her name was Keturah and she bore to him..."

Isaac and Rebekah's marriage Gen 24:64 The hebrew words say, "...bo Yitschaq ohel Sarah em laqach eth Ribqah hayah low ishshah aheb..." which translates "...and brought her Isaac (he laughs) into the tent of Sarah his mother and took Rebekah and she became his wife..."

There are more positives to changing wedding tradition to this biblical acceptance of marriage;

1) People (believers) would take VERY seriously having "premarital" sex if they believed that having sex was getting married. "Premarital" sex in the church is a very serious problem. Why? No consequences. If the Church started preaching that the sexual union was marriage wouldn't more people curtail that behavior until they found the person they wanted to marry?

2) The problems today with "homosexual marriage" would not even exist if we just paid attention to God's simple definition of marriage. It says the male and female choose to leave and cleave and what God put together let no one separate. If the church did not add to these verses to include pastors (or the state) giving the okay, then there could not be any homosexual marriage. God clearly states the MALE and FEMALE unite. But now the homosexuals have a valid point because of the licensing and sanctioning process that the church is willingly participating in!

3) Non-christians would see that christians are giving God the recognition that he invented sex and giving Him all the glory for uniting the husband and wife. "...what God put together (let no man separate)..." This is very important because it puts the attention back on God rather than the pomp and ceremony performed in front of people and pastors who initiate unbiblical decrees- "I now pronounce you man and wife", or "you may now kiss the bride".

Last note (for now); I'm still researching this topic and looking into the bible's original words for many subjects such as; "to know"- meaning having sex

Written in love, with no malice and great appreciation of your thoughts, Brad

** After this email exchange it was suggested that, if what I was saying were true, then someone who rapes another would be married to them (since it is a union of the bodies). Biblically this is not so. God's word specifically says that the two people getting married CHOOSE to leave their mother and father. In a rape situation, one person is forced and is not choosing.

Notes

Chapter 3: LOVE

1. *What's Love Got to Do With It*. By Tina Turner, 1984.
2. Shakespeare, William. *A Midnight Summer's Dream*. New York, Dover Publications, 1992.
3. Dostoyevsky, Fyodor. *The Brothers Karamazov*. Penguin Books, 2003.
4. Lewis, C.S. *The Four Loves*. Harcourt Books, 1960.
5. Dawkins, Richard. Letter. 20 Sept. 2006.
6. *True Love*. By P!nk, 2012.
7. Bernieres, Louis De. *Captain Corelli's Mandolin*. New York, Pantheon Books, 1994.

Chapter 6: My Answer is No

1. *Any Man of Mine*. By Shania Twain, 1995.

Chapter 7: Spread **** on their Face (Malachi 2:3)

1. "George Carlin - They are only WORDS!" *Youtube*, 8 Apr. 2011, www.youtube.com/watch?v=mUvdXxhLPa8.

Chapter 8: Non-Christians... meh

1. "John Cleese: Political Correctness Can Lead to an Orwellian Nightmare." *Youtube*, 31 Jan. 2016, www.youtube.com/watch?v=QAK0KXEpF8U.

2.   Newkirk, Ingrid in *Vogue Magazine*. 1 Sept. 1989

3.   Milian, Jorge. "Five malnourished children found living in car at Greenacres Walmart." *Palmbeachpost.com*, 21 Dec. 2016, www.palmbeachpost.com/news/crime--law/five-malnourished-children-found-living-car-greenacres-walmart/Dc wYX2sM2pp6DzwHLV8UYN/.

4.   LaBeouf, Shia. "Film Shia LaBeouf." Interview by Elvis Mitchell. *Interview*, 20 Oct. 2014.

Chapter 9: Scientists Suck Too

1.   Dawkins, Richard. Letter. 20 Sept. 2006.

2.   Dawkins, Richard. *River Out of Eden: A Darwinian View of Life*. Basic Books, 1995.

Chapter 10: Nature Never Goes Out of Style

1.   Keats, John. "On the Grasshopper and Cricket." 1816. *The Poetical Works of John Keats*, 1884.

2.   Plath, Sylvia. *The Bell Jar*. Harper and Row Publishers, 1971.

3.   Holmes, Reginald Vincent. "The Magic of Sound." 1955. *Fireside Fancies*, Edward Brothers, 1955.

4.   "Ralph Waldo Emerson Quotes." *Good Reads*, www.goodreads.com/quotes/20326-adopt-the-pace-of-nature-her-secret-is-patience.

5.   "Abraham Lincoln Quotes." *Good Reads*, www.goodreads.com/quotes/131220-i-can-see-how-it-might-be-possible-for-a.